The Trail of Blood:

Sacrifice in the Quran and the Bible—
from Adam to the Throne

by
Don McCurry

Published 2018
Ministries to Muslims

GLOBAL INITIATIVE
REACHING **MUSLIM** PEOPLES

Global Initiative possesses all rights, titles, and interests.
Please contact them directly for permission and coordination
for use, translation, or distribution:

contact@reachingmuslimpeoples.com

Acknowledgements

First and foremost, I must thank the Lord God Almighty, who is One, for His great love and compassion for me. I am humbled by His care and delight.

For my wife of seventy years, Mary Jo, whose faithful love and humility has been a source of incredible strength and stability for me. Thank you with all my love and affection!

For all the men and women throughout my life that have been used by God to model for me the qualities and reality of God so that I might know Him ever better. Thank you!

For the men on my Board who have consistently served to help me stay focused upon God's call for me and provide support in more ways than I can ever begin to enumerate. Thank you!

For my very gracious friends who have generously donated the funds needed to begin and complete this project. Thank you!

And my special thanks for Gayle W. Herde, Ph.D., and her husband and MTM board member, Bryan Herde, who have co-labored with me in bringing this book into reality and making it available to all who desire to journey with me along the trail of blood.

Introduction

And We ransomed him with a mighty sacrifice…
Quran 37:107

"God will provide for Himself the lamb for a burnt offering…"
Genesis 22:8 (O.T.)

Sacrifice is a powerful term used repeatedly throughout the Quran and the Bible. These two excerpts above both refer to a critical moment in the life of Abraham when a sacrifice of tremendous importance was occurring.

Consequently, we have been compelled to take a thorough look into the correlation between these two statements, among scores of others from both the Quran and the Bible, in order to understand the significance of sacrifice.

It is our hope that you are reading this book because you, too, desire to learn and consider what the Quran teaches, as well as what the Quran calls "the Book," "the Scriptures" or "the Gospel" (or what is more commonly known as the Bible), teaches about sacrifice.

Please walk patiently with us down this "trail of blood" as together we look carefully at many powerful and relevant statements that shed more light upon our journeys throughout this life and beyond.

Author's Notes

As in many books of this sort, we feel it is necessary to set forth some of our assumptions and conventions.

First and foremost, as this book is a comparison of material in both the Bible and the Quran, we have written this not just for Westerners who have English as their mother tongue, but also for many in our audience whose mother tongue is Arabic or some other related language.

We also assume that with many readers there is a lack of familiarity with the content and format of the Bible. We explain some of the things that people accustomed to Western publications perhaps take for granted. We have no desire to "talk down" to anyone; instead, we hope to avoid any potential misunderstandings that could be perceived as lack of cultural sensitivity:

- The Bible (occasionally called "the Ancient Scriptures," "Scriptures," or "the Book"), like the Quran, is made up of very many subdivisions. In the Quran, they are called suras; in the Bible, they are called books. Therefore, the Bible is a book made up of many smaller books. Those books are divided into chapters, which are further divided (like the Quran) into verses. There will be reminders of this sprinkled throughout this text.

- When we give the reference for materials from the Bible (and it is our hope and expectation that you will check these for yourself), we will list first the name of the book, then the chapter, then the verse or range of verses. For example, John 3:16-17 would indicate the New Testament book of John, the third chapter and the sixteenth and seventeenth verses. When only part of a verse is used, generally "a" (first portion) or "b" (second portion) might appear in the reference.

- We should also mention that the Bible is divided into two major sections: the Old Testament and the New Testament. The Old Testament (occasionally called the Old Covenant) covers the period of the time from creation through 400 years preceding the birth of Jesus. The New Testament (or New Covenant) begins slightly before the birth of Jesus and continues through the end of the first century (by Western reckoning), with one additional book of prophecy that addresses events yet to occur in the undetermined future. Also, for our readers unfamiliar with where the books are located within the Bible, we will indicate in the text whether they are Old (O.T.) or New (N.T.) Testament. We have also listed the books of the Bible in order in the Appendix. We hope you find this helpful.

- Western publications have certain guidelines when it comes to exactly quoting material from other sources. Short quotations generally remain within the narrative text, while longer quotations are indented. References are given for all direct quotations.

- When material is being quoted exactly, the author will sometimes add helpful or explanatory material. That material generally appears in square brackets [ ] to distinguish it from the quoted material. Explanatory material within the ordinary narrative will appear in parentheses ( ).

- The Bible is full of poetry, whether in songs of praise or lament, or in prophecy, or when being quoted by someone within the Bible. In the case of longer poetry, it is indented and the lines appear as they do in the original. With smaller poetic quotations, a slash (/) will appear between lines.

- Summaries by the author (and there are a substantial number of summaries) of material in the Bible or Quran will be contained within the narrative, so as not to be confused with direct quotations.

- We have chosen to use the older terms BC and AD, rather than BCE and CE, as well as the Western calculation and format for naming years (for example, 2018 AD).

- Finally, we feel it is important to mention an "outdated" convention with which we are in disagreement: In earlier times, references to God were capitalized out of reverence. That is now considered obsolete, in part because the original manuscripts did not contain capital letters. We disagree and out of respect will continue to capitalize the most common pronouns (He, Him, His, etc.) dealing with God in the Bible. It's the least we can do.

Table of Contents

Chapter 1

A Brief History of the Quran

The early followers of Islam were taught to memorize the words of the Quran.[1] We have also learned from history that some passages were written on parchments, on white stones, on the broad, dried bones of animals, and on the dried parts of palm leaves. This was the situation in 632 AD, when the Prophet died.

When Abu Bakr was elected caliph of Islam in 632, he gave the order to a young secretary, Zayd Ibn Thabit, to collect what was written, integrate it with the best oral recitation, and codify it in manuscript form. When Abu Bakr died in 634 the manuscript was given to the next caliph, Umar, for safe-keeping. It was kept under the bed of his widowed daughter for eleven years until he was assassinated. It was then given to the third caliph, Uthman. During his reign, rival generals of widely separated armies had, through oral transmission, recited versions of the Quran and began feuding over whose version was the right one. To avoid civil war, Caliph Uthman appointed four men to agree on the official version. Then after this process was completed, all divergent versions were destroyed.

---

[1] Quran means "Recitations."

The official version of the Quran was written with no vowels, only consonants. As official copies were sent to various parts of the empire, a new problem arose. Men reciting the Quran, separated geographically, used their local pronunciation. This situation continued for 150 years, resulting in ten accepted versions. This problem was finally solved when a group of scholars agreed to put vowels in the words. Until this happened, a word spelled without vowels was subject to many different meanings, thereby compromising the text; they chose one official copy from that time forward.

Also, for any readers who are not familiar with how the Quran is arranged, it is divided into chapters, known as suras, that have been given both numbers and names (for example, "The Cow," "The Night-Journey," and so on), then further divided into numbered verses. We will use the initial "Q." throughout this work to indicate their source as the Quran, as well as the sura and verse numbers.

When we read the official version of the Quran, we discover that there are many stories that are common to both the Quran and the earlier Scriptures, ordinarily called the Bible.[2]

In order to establish the continuity between the Quran and Bible, there are many verses in the Quran that affirm the Bible. We are now going to look at a few of them for assurance that it is permissible for a Muslim to read the Bible.

---

[2] "Bible" simply means "book."

Chapter 2

The Bible Affirmed by the
Quran and Other Sources

There are two books on which our work is based: the Quran and the Bible. For a Muslim reader of this study, the Quran needs no explanation; other readers unacquainted with the Quran, please refer to the previous chapter. For those who are not familiar with the Bible, which pre-dated the Quran by many hundreds of years, a word of explanation may be helpful.

The first portion of the Bible, the Old Covenant, more commonly called the Old Testament (O.T.), is comprised of thirty-nine books of various lengths. The word "covenant" refers to a pledge God made with people He chose for His purposes in the world. Together these books describe human history from Adam to the four-hundred year-period prior to the time of Christ and include twenty-one persons who are common to both the Quran and the Old Testament.[3]

The second portion of the Bible, the New Covenant, or the New Testament (N.T.), is a collection of twenty-seven

---

[3] A list of these Old Testament books is found in the Appendix. Note that some of these books were divided into multiple volumes, such as the first and second book of the kings, for example, written as "1 Kings" and "2 Kings.")

books.[4] It includes the Gospels, four in number, the Acts of Jesus' disciples, followed by a series of instructions in letter form to churches and individuals, and finally a very unusual book called "The Revelation of Jesus Christ." Two of the Gospels were written by men who associated face to face with Jesus for three years; two other Gospels are believed to have been written on behalf of other direct followers.

Together, the collection of these thirty-nine books in the Old Testament and twenty-seven books in the New Testament, sixty-six books in all, are put together under one cover called the Bible. The Old Testament was written over a period of time from 1,400 years to 400 years before Christ. The New Testament was written by eyewitnesses in the period after Christ's ascension to heaven. Altogether, these writings covered 1,500 years written by forty known Holy Spirit-inspired authors.

These are the inspired Scriptures that are referred to in the Quran. On the following pages are listed a few Quranic references affirming the Bible.

Quranic Affirmations of Scripture

The Quran (the Recitations) confirms the Law of Moses (the *Tawrat* or Torah), all the prophets and their books, and the Gospel (*Injil* or "Good News") given to Jesus. There can be no change in the Word of God (Q. 10:64).

---

[4] A list of these New Testament books is found in the Appendix. Note that some of the letters of instruction were written in response to questions from the recipients, so we have, as an example, the first and second letter of Peter, the apostle, shown as "1 Peter" and "2 Peter."

This includes the Old and New Testament. Christians and Jews are chided for not obeying the teaching of their own books, and Christians, specifically, are exhorted to stand on their own Scriptures.

Please note: The Prophet of Islam, as far as we know, never saw the real Bible, especially in his own language. He was exposed to Jewish commentaries and to apocryphal[5] Gnostic gospels of the third and fourth centuries after Christ[6]. The one possible exception is material from Luke's gospel in the Quran that is not in the Gnostic Gospels. This was possibly brought back from Ethiopia by his followers who fled there temporarily for protection from the Meccan pagans.

Here are some of the Quranic materials affirming the Bible:

> Say ye: "We believe in Allah, and in what has been revealed to us and what was revealed to Abraham, Isma'il, Isaac, Jacob, and the Tribes, and in (the Books) given to Moses, Jesus, and the Prophets, from their Lord. We make no distinction between one and another among them, and to Allah do we bow our will (in Islam).
> Q. 3:84 (Also see the same quotation in Q. 2:136.)

> It was We who revealed the Law (to Moses): Therein was guidance and light. By its standards

---

[5] "Apocryphal" means "of doubtful authenticity, although widely circulated as being true."

[6] This is a title for Jesus taken from the Greek word, "Christos." Many times, the Bible refers to Jesus simply as "Christ." See chapter 19 for more on this.

have been judged the Jews, by the Prophets who bowed (as in Islam) to Allah's Will…
Q. 5:44

And in their footsteps [the prophets'] We sent Jesus the son of Mary, confirming the Law that had come before him: We sent him the Gospel: Therein was guidance and light, and confirmation of the Law that had come before him: A guidance and an admonition to those who fear Allah. Let the People of the Gospel judge by what Allah hath revealed therein. If any do fail to judge by (the light of) what Allah hath revealed, they are (no better than) those who rebel.
Q. 5:46-47

If only they [the Jews and the Christians] had stood fast by the Law, the Gospel [*Injil*] and all the revelation that was sent to them from their Lord, they would enjoyed happiness from every side…"
Say: "O People of the Book [Jews and Christians], Ye have no ground to stand upon unless ye stand fast by the Law, the Gospel, and all the revelation that has come to you from your Lord."
Q. 5:66, 68

[T]here is none that can alter the words and decrees of Allah.
Q. 6:34

[The Quran] is a confirmation of (revelations) that went before it.
Q. 10:37

No change can there be in the words of Allah.
Q. 10:64

If thou wert in doubt as to what We have revealed
unto thee, then ask those [Christians and Jews] who
have been reading the Book [Old and New
Testaments] from before thee: the Truth hath
indeed come to thee from thy Lord...
Q. 10:94

That which We have revealed to thee of the Book
[the Bible] is the Truth—confirming what was
(revealed) before it: For Allah is assuredly—with
respect to His servants—well acquainted and Fully-
Observant. Then We have given the Book for
inheritance to such of Our servants as We have
chosen...
Q. 35:31-32

And before this was the Book of Moses as a guide
and a mercy: and this Book confirms (it) in the
Arabic tongue...
Q. 46:12

We [Allah] sent Noah and Abraham, and
established in their line Prophethood and
Revelation:...We sent after them Jesus [*Isa*] son of
Mary, and bestowed on him the Gospel [*Injil*] and
We ordained in the hearts of those who followed
him Compassion and Mercy...
Q. 57:26-27

Biblical Self-Affirmation of Scripture

In the same way, the Scripture is self-referential as to its own inerrancy, accuracy, truth, and application.

> Blessed is the man…(whose) delight is in the law of the Lord, and on His law he meditates day and night…his leaf does not wither. In all that he does he prospers.
> Psalm 1:1-3 (O.T)

> Your word is a lamp to my feet and a light to my path…The unfolding of Your words gives light; it imparts understanding to the simple.
> Psalm 119:105, 130 (O.T.)

> [T]ake…the sword of the Spirit, which is the Word of God…
> Ephesians 6:17 (N.T.)

> Let the word of Christ dwell in you richly, teaching and admonishing one another in all wisdom…
> Colossians 3:16a (N.T.)

> All Scripture is breathed out by God and is profitable for teaching, for reproof, for correction, and for training in righteousness, that the man of God may be complete, equipped for every good work.
> 2 Timothy 3:16-17 (N.T.)

Do your best to present yourself to God as one approved, a worker who has no need to be ashamed, rightly handling the word of truth.
2 Timothy 2:15 (N.T.)

For the word of God is living and active, sharper than any two-edged sword, piercing to the division of soul and spirit, of joints and of marrow, and discerning the thoughts and intentions of the heart. And no creature is hidden from His sight, but all are naked and exposed to the eyes of Him to whom we must give account.
Hebrews 4:12-13 (N.T.)

[K]nowing this first of all, that no prophecy of Scripture comes from someone's own interpretation. For no prophecy was ever produced by the will of man, but men spoke from God as they were carried along by the Holy Spirit.
2 Peter 1:20-21 (N.T.)

Remarkably, even Satan himself, the great enemy of God and humankind, quoted from the Scriptures when it suited his need. It is important to observe, however, that he misused the Scriptures and was soundly corrected by Jesus in the gospel of Matthew, chapter 4, verses 5 through 7 (N.T.):

Then the devil took Him [Jesus] to the holy city and set Him on the pinnacle of the temple, and said to Him, "If You are the Son of God, throw Yourself down, for it is written, "He will command His angels concerning You," and "On their hands they will bear you up, lest You strike Your foot against a stone'" [misquoting Psalm 91:11-12]. Jesus said to him, "Again it is written: Do not put the Lord your God to the test" [Deuteronomy 6:16, O.T.].

Jesus, about whom more will be said later in this work, affirmed the importance of the Scriptures:

But He [Jesus] answered "Man shall not live by bread alone, but by every Word that comes from the mouth of God."
Matthew 4:4 (N.T.)

"Do not think that I [Jesus] have come to abolish the Law and the Prophets; I have not come to abolish them but to fulfill them. For truly, I say to you, until heaven and earth pass away, not an iota, not a dot, will pass from the Law until all is accomplished."
Matthew 5:17-18 (N.T.)

"Heaven and earth will pass away, but My [Jesus'] words will not pass away."
Mark 13:31 (N.T.)

So Jesus said…"If you abide in My word, you are truly My disciples, and you will know the truth and the truth will set you free."
John 8:31-32 (N.T.)

"If you abide in Me [Jesus], and My words abide in you, ask whatever you wish, and it will be done for you."
John 15:7 (N.T.)

Other Affirmations of Scripture

Finally, objective, secular guidelines have been put forth for anyone genuinely interested in determining the authenticity and accuracy of documents handed down from ancient times, including the Bible. Questions to be answered include:

- Was this work written by the person(s) purported to have written it? [7]

- Was it written at the time alleged to be the date of composition?

- Was it written under the circumstances and for the purpose alleged?

The data required for answering the questions above include the following:

- Bibliographic evidence refers to the materials used to create the document. For example, are the writing materials, use of language, idioms, sentence structure, etc. appropriate for the time period?

- Does the alleged author(s) make a claim to have written the material within the document or in other verified materials?

- External evidence is derived from an examination of historical or biographical events, or statements made by persons with personal or near-personal

---

[7] See Sanders, Chauncey. *An Introduction to Research in English Literary History.* The MacMillan Co: NY. 1952. P. 143-161.

knowledge of the author(s) or the work(s), among other items.

- Internal evidence is necessary. For example, are the style, vocabulary, subject matter, opinions expressed, literary style, and so on consistent with the purported author(s)?

Academically speaking, the benefit of the doubt generally is given in favor of the genuineness of the document. To prove a document has been altered, it should be compared against the original and shown to be deficient. There should be evidence demonstrating who made the change and when. Large numbers of identical copies give strength to the conclusion of accuracy.

Literally thousands of fragments and documents support the accuracy of the Bible, and more are being discovered every year. These can be viewed in major, world-class, reputable museums and are also held in private collections. Some of the New Testament manuscripts have even been carbon-dated to the same century within which Jesus lived, and Old Testament manuscripts are even older.

These earliest fragments have been found to be valid, certified, and beautifully accurate, showing them to be free from corruption. The Bible, comprised of the Old Testament and the New Testament, and affirmed by the Quran, can be trusted.

Chapter 3

Satan

We all acknowledge that there is evil in the world. Its presence is everywhere, evident in all cultures, among all peoples, and in all lands. Evil has an origin, it has a cause, it has a father, and his name is Satan. He is the author of all sin and the father of lies. He despises God and all that God does and is.

Satan, *"Iblis"* or *"Shaitan"* in Arabic, is the enemy of every man, woman and child on this planet. Both the Quran and the Bible address him and those evil beings associated with him. It is important that we understand this contrary force working in the world against the plans and will of God.

In the Quran

> Then did Satan make them slip from the (garden), and get them out of the state (of felicity) in which they had been.
> Q. 2:36

> Their (real) wish is to resort together for judgment (in their disputes) to the Evil One, though they

were ordered to reject him. But Satan's wish is to lead them astray far away (from the right).
Q. 4:60

So fight ye against the friends of Satan: feeble indeed is the cunning of Satan.
Q. 4:76

Were it not for the Grace and Mercy of Allah unto you, all but a few of you would have followed Satan.
Q. 4:83

(The Pagans), leaving Him, call but upon female deities: They call but upon Satan the persistent rebel!
Q. 4:117

Allah did curse him [Satan], but he said: "I will take of Thy servants a portion marked off; I will mislead them, and I will create in them false desires; I will order them to slit the ears of cattle, and to deface the (fair) nature created by Allah." Whoever, forsaking Allah, takes Satan for a friend, hath of a surety suffered a loss that is manifest. Satan makes them promises and creates in them false desires; but Satan's promises are nothing but deception. They (his dupes) will have their dwelling in Hell, and from it they will find no way of escape.
Q. 4:118-121

In the Bible: Satan's Fall from Heaven

There was a war in heaven because Satan determined to exalt himself above God. One-third of the angels joined Satan in his rebellion, were defeated and cast out of Heaven or imprisoned. Those fallen angels are called demons. The following verses provide some insights into this event:

> "How you are fallen from heaven, O Day Star, son of Dawn [Lucifer, Satan]! How you are cut down to the ground, you who laid the nations low! You said in your heart, 'I will ascend to heaven; above the stars of God I will set my throne on high; I will sit on the mount of assembly in the far reaches of the north; I will ascend above the heights of the clouds; I will make myself like the Most High.' But you are brought down to Sheol [Hell], to the far reaches of the pit."
> Isaiah 14:12-15 (O.T.)

We read in Ezekiel 28:12-17 (O.T.) that Satan is the spirit being behind the throne of Tyre, the signet of perfection—beautiful; the anointed guardian cherub. Unrighteousness was found in him. His heart was proud because of his beauty. He was cast to the ground.

In Revelation 12:3-4, 7-9 (N.T.), Satan is thrown out of Heaven down to the Earth with one-third of the angels with him—those who rebelled against God.

In Jude 1:6 (N.T.) we find that many of those angels are kept in chains awaiting judgment.

Satan and Demons on Earth

[A]nd the whole world lies in the power of the evil one [Satan].
1 John 5:19 (N.T.)

"He [Satan] was a murderer from the beginning, and does not stand in the truth, because there is no truth in him. When he lies, he speaks out of his own character, for he is a liar and the father of lies."
John 8:44 (N.T.)

Now the serpent [Satan] was more crafty than any other beast of the field that the Lord God had made. He said to the woman, "Did God actually say, 'You shall not eat of any tree in the garden?'" And the woman said to the serpent, "We may eat of the fruit of the trees in the garden, but God said, 'You shall not eat of the fruit of the tree that is in the midst of the garden, neither shall you touch it, lest you die.'" "You will not surely die. For God knows that when you eat of it your eyes will be opened, and you will be like God, knowing good and evil." So when the woman saw that the tree was good for food, and that it was a delight to the eyes, and that the tree was to be desired to make one wise, she took of its fruit and ate, and she also gave some to her husband who was with her, and he ate. Then the eyes of both were opened, and they knew that they were naked.
Genesis 3:1-7 (O.T.)

Then the Lord God said to the woman, "What is this that you have done?"

The woman said, "The serpent deceived me, and I ate."

So the Lord God said to the serpent,

"Because you have done this, cursed are you above all livestock

and above all beasts of the field;

on your belly you shall go,

and dust you shall eat

all the days of your life. I will put enmity between you and the woman,

and between your offspring and her offspring;

He shall bruise your head,

and you shall bruise His heel."

Genesis 3:13-15 (O.T.)

Then Jesus was led up by the Spirit into the wilderness to be tempted by the devil. And after fasting forty days and forty nights, He was hungry. And the tempter came and said to Him, "If you are the Son of God, command these stones to become loaves of bread." But He answered, "It is written,

'Man shall not live by bread alone,

but by every word that comes from the mouth of God.'"

Then the devil took Him to the holy city and set Him on the pinnacle of the Temple and said to Him, "If you are the Son of God, throw yourself down, for it is written,

'He will command his angels concerning you,'

and

> 'On their hands they will bear you up, lest
> you strike your foot against a stone.'"

Jesus said to him, "Again it is written, 'You shall not put the Lord your God to the test.'" Again, the devil took Him to a very high mountain and showed Him all the kingdoms of the world and their glory. And he said to Him, "All these I will give you, if you will fall down and worship me." Then Jesus said to him, "Be gone, Satan! For it is written,

> 'You shall worship the Lord your God and
> Him only shall you serve.'"

Then the devil left him, and behold, angels came and were ministering to Him.
Matthew 4:1-11 (N.T.)

When he [a demon-possessed man] saw Jesus, he cried out and fell down before Him and said with a loud voice, 'What have You to do with me, Jesus, Son of the Most High God? I beg You, do not torment me.' For He had commanded the unclean spirit to come out of the man. (For many a time it had seized him. He was kept under guard and bound with chains and shackles, but he would break the bonds and be driven by the demon into the desert.) Jesus then asked him, 'What is your name?' And he said, 'Legion,' for many demons had entered him. And they begged Him not to command them to depart into the abyss.
Luke 8:28-31 (N.T.)

While he was coming, the demon threw him [a man's son] to the ground and convulsed him. But

Jesus rebuked the unclean spirit [demon] and
healed the boy...
Luke 9:42 (N.T.)

Now He [Jesus] was casting out a demon that was
mute. When the demon had gone out, the mute
man spoke, and the people marveled.
Luke 11:14 (N.T.)

Commentary

Certainly, all humankind has a powerful enemy, Satan,
who uses lies, deceit, and trickery to ensure his grip on
hearts and lives so that people will never come to the
knowledge of the truth about him, the world and sin. He
causes pain, suffering and intense hatred for all that God is
and all that God loves.

However, God is not mocked, nor is His sovereignty
threatened by an enemy that is as forceful as Satan. Even
Satan is answerable to God. But we can be aware of his
devices and of his capacity to be weakened, overcome and,
ultimately, defeated in every way for all eternity. Jesus was
given that ability while He walked this planet and was
given authority over Satan and his dominion. More about
this will be discussed later in this book.

Chapter 4

Sacrifice

Sin is costly. It is destructive and harmful. It is the opposite of God. God cannot ignore sin. Only an extreme act that involves the shedding of blood, the taking of a life, could come close to approximating the seriousness of offending a holy and perfectly pure God. Sacrifice is required for forgiveness to be granted by God to anyone who repents.

Throughout history, people of various nations, cultures and locations have ritually offered sacrifices of one kind or another to their own deities either for forgiveness for what they have done, to appease their deities' anger, or to seek special favors.

But the One True God has a different view and purpose for why sacrifices are essential. Let's find out what He requires.

In the Quran

There are four words in Arabic to indicate sacrifice or an animal that is slain as an offering. Listed below are those words with illustrations from their use in the Quran:

Zebeeh

> And remember Moses said to his people: "Allah commands that ye sacrifice a heifer."
> Q. 2:67

> [Abraham] said "O my son! I see in vision that I offer thee in sacrifice…"
> Q. 37:102

Qurban

> "…He showed us a sacrifice consumed by fire."
> Q. 3:183

> Behold! They each [Cain and Abel] presented a sacrifice.
> Q. 5:27

Nahr

> Therefore to thy Lord turn in Prayer and Sacrifice.
> Q. 108:2

> So when ye have accomplished your holy rites, celebrate the praises of Allah…. [These holy rites include animal sacrifices.]
> Q. 2:200

> To every people did We appoint rites (of sacrifice) …He gave them from animals (fit for food)…
> Q. 22:34

Hady

> …send an offering for sacrifice…
> Q. 2:196

Violate not the sanctity of the Symbols of Allah…
nor of the animals brought for sacrifice…
Q. 5:2

In orthodox Islam, there are two occasions when Muslims
are instructed to make sacrifices. The first is at *Eid al
Azha*, which occurs on the tenth day of the lunar month
of *Zul al Hijjah*. The other occasion is on the birth of a
child during the ceremony of *Aqiqah*.

What is of interest in this study is that once a year during
Eid al Azha, blood flows all over the Muslim world as
animals are slaughtered by the millions. On this day, at
least one hundred million animals are killed.

The *Aqiqah* rite is observed with animal sacrifices offered
for every Muslim child that is born (usually two for a boy
and one for a girl). When Muslim children are born, blood
is shed in observing this ceremony.

In the Bible

Throughout the Bible, various words have been used for
"sacrifice," first in the Old Testament in the Hebrew
language, and then in the Greek language in the New
Testament.

Zebach refers to an animal that has been slaughtered for
ritual sacrifice. Examples are given from many periods of
history, including:

Jacob [*Yaqoob*] offered a sacrifice [of an animal] in the hill country and called his kinsmen to eat bread.
Genesis 31:54 (O.T.)

…Moses' father-in-law brought a burnt offering and sacrifices to God.
Exodus 18:12 (O.T.)

The flesh of the sacrifice of his peace offerings for thanksgiving shall be eaten on that day of his offering.
Leviticus 7:15 (O.T.)

Offer right sacrifices and put your trust in the Lord.
Psalms (*Zabur* in Arabic) 4:5 (O.T)

Chag (festal sacrifice)
The Lord is God, and He has made His light to shine upon us. Bind the festal sacrifice with cords…
Psalm 118:27 (O.T)

Minchah (offering)
At the evening sacrifice I rose from my fasting…and fell upon my knees and spread out my hands to the Lord my God.
Ezra (*Uzair*) 9:5 (O.T)

Ishsheh (sacrifice by fire)
You shall offer a burnt offering…with a pleasing aroma to the Lord.
Numbers 29:13 (O.T.)

Thusia (slaughtered animal)

> [A]s it is written in the Law of the Lord, "Every male who first opens the womb shall be called holy to the Lord"…offer a sacrifice according to what is said in the Law of the Lord.
> Luke 2:23-24 (N.T.)

> By faith Abel (*Habeel*) offered to God a more acceptable sacrifice than Cain (*Qabeel*), through which he was commended as righteous.
> Hebrews 11:4 (N.T.)

Theu (to sacrifice)

> Christ, our Passover lamb, has been sacrificed.
> 1 Corinthians 5:7 (N.T.)

Occasionally, there are instances in the Bible of people building altars without explicitly stating that a sacrifice was made upon it. However, the first time that the Bible uses the term "altar" is in the story of Noah. After the flood, after the water receded, and the earth dried enough to support life again, it is said, "Then Noah built an altar to the Lord and took some of every clean animal and some of every clean bird and offered burnt offerings on the altar (Genesis 8:20, O.T.). The word "altar" comes from the Hebrew word *misbeah* meaning "altar," which in turn comes from a primitive root word, *zabah*, meaning "to *slaughter* an animal (usually in sacrifice)." Therefore, in looking at the original language, the words "altar" and "sacrifice" are inextricably linked in practice.

Sacrifice requires the shedding of blood. The meaning and purpose for blood is significant for those who want to know and understand God.

Chapter 5

Blood

Blood is life. When it is shed in sacrifice, it is a significant act and one that has meanings that are important to understand.

In the Quran

Let's start with what the Quran has to say:

> Behold, thy Lord said to the angels: "I will create a vicegerent[8] on the earth." They said: "Wilt Thou place therein one who will make mischief therein and shed blood?..."
> Q. 2:30

> And remember We took your Covenant (to this effect): Shed no blood amongst you...
> Q. 2:84

---

[8] This is not a misspelling, just a very uncommon word with similar spelling to "vice-regent." It is a deputy appointed to act on the authority of a ruler or magistrate, especially in administrative duties.

He hath only forbidden you dead meat, and blood, and the flesh of swine.
Q. 2:173

Forbidden to you (for food) are dead meat, blood, the flesh of swine...
Q. 5:3

Say: "I find not in the Message received by me by inspiration any (meat) forbidden to be eaten by one who wishes to eat it, unless it be dead meat, or blood poured forth, or the flesh of swine—for it is an abomination..."
Q. 6:145

So We sent (plagues) on them: Wholesale Death, Locusts, Lice, Frogs, and Blood: signs openly self-explained...
Q. 7:133

He has only forbidden you dead meat, and blood, and the flesh of swine...
Q. 16:115

It is not their meat nor their blood that reaches Allah: it is your piety that reaches Him...
Q. 22:37

In the Bible

When one looks at the list of all the verses in the Bible that mention blood, well, it is a bit overwhelming. If you were to count all the times blood is mentioned in the

Bible, it comes to 436. If you tried to locate them all, you would find them in forty-one of the sixty-six books of the Bible. While the writing of the Bible covered a period of 1,500 years (1400 BC to 100 AD), the period of the shedding of blood ended when the Jewish Temple was destroyed in 70 AD.

As we look back through human history, all the way back to the first human family, we know that the first human ever born killed his brother—shed his blood. And to this day, human history is still the same: humans kill humans. This raises several more important questions:

- Were there not laws prohibiting the shedding of blood?

- If it was against the will of God to murder, then what is the punishment for such a crime?

- In a wider sense, shouldn't there be a punishment for doing something against the will of God (also known as rebellion)?

The answer is yes. The final punishment for rebellion against God at any point is death, as stated in Romans 6:23 (N.T.), "For the wages of sin is death..." Can even one person claim to have lived a life perfectly free from any sin? If we're honest, the answer would have to be no. This is clearly communicated in Romans 3:23 (N.T.), "[F]or all have sinned and fall short of the glory of God." And since we all agree that all have sinned and earned death, what hope then is there for us? Did God create a way for us to be saved from such a dreadful fate? The answer again is yes.

In almost every book in the Bible and with all the chapters of the Quran, save one, we read of God that He is merciful and compassionate. That fact lies at the very heart of this book you are reading now.

Without exception, this book is about God. He is just. He does punish. Is He also compassionate? Yes. Since a sinner cannot save himself or herself, then help has to come from God Himself. There is no other conclusion.

> As it is written: "None is righteous, no, not one; no one understands; no one seeks for God. All have turned aside; together they have become worthless; no one does good, not even one." "Their throat is an open grave; they use their tongues to deceive." "The venom of asps is under their lips." "Their mouth is full of curses and bitterness." "Their feet are swift to shed blood; in their paths are ruin and misery, and the way of peace they have not known." "There is no fear of God before their eyes."…For all have sinned and fall short of the glory of God.
> Romans 3:10-18, 23 (N.T.)

Rather than get into a heavy discussion on theology about God, we will confine our studies to stories—stories that are common to both the Bible and the Quran—stories of how God relates to human beings. Let us see what we can learn about the character of God and how He solves this problem for all human beings—the problem of sin and the arrangement for the forgiveness of sin. To do so, we will study familiar men who are mentioned in the Quran and the Bible.

The study begins with Adam and his wife. Together with Adam and Eve, we shall also encounter Satan and his role in this long drama. As we continue, we intend to study how God related to Adam's two sons, Cain and Abel, then Noah, Abraham, Isaac, Ishmael, Jacob, Job, David, Solomon, Elijah, Elisha, Jonah, Isaiah, Malachi, Zachariah, John the Baptist, Mary, and Jesus. We will also refer to the testimonies of the disciples Matthew, John, Peter and Paul and another book of the New Testament called Hebrews, whose author we do not know. These all will contribute to our theme of the trail of blood from Adam to the throne.

Chapter 6

Adam

Both the Quran and the Bible tell the story of mankind's beginning. The account in the book of Genesis ("the Book of Beginnings," O.T.) was written a little more than 2,000 years before the Quran was written down. In both accounts, Adam is the first man created by God and is therefore the perfect person with whom to begin.

In the Quran

The Quran is a collection of utterances and was not written in chronological order.[9] So the story of Adam and Eve (*Hawa*) does not occur in the beginning of the Quran; in fact, different versions of the Adam and Eve story are scattered throughout many chapters of the Quran. Following is a summary of the relevant material.

Allah told the angels that He was going to create man as a ruler on the earth. The angels asked Allah why he was going to create a being that would cause mischief on the earth and shed blood. Allah's reply was that he knew

---

[9] Please see "History of the Quran" for more information.

things the angels didn't. And so, Adam was created out of dust, by one account, out of mud or clay in another, and out of congealed blood in another. Allah breathed his spirit into him. Allah taught Adam the names of everything. Allah appointed for him the seasons of life, including the time he would die. Originally, Allah put him in a garden with his wife, and told him not to go near "the" tree lest he run into harm or transgression. (Q. 2:30-33, 35)

Allah ordered all the angels to worship Adam, but *Iiblis* (*Shaitan*, the devil, Satan) refused, saying, in his pride, that he was superior to Adam since he was made of fire and Adam was made of dust. When Satan refused to worship Adam, God told him to get down (out of the garden down to the earth). But before Satan was expelled from the garden, he caused Adam to slip from his estate there. He whispered to Adam and Eve that Allah did not want them to eat of this tree because they would become like the angels and live forever. By deceit he caused their fall. When they tasted of the tree, they became aware of their shame. They sewed leaves to cover their bodies. Allah appeared and said, "Did not I warn you that Satan was your avowed enemy?" Adam and his wife confessed that they had wronged their own souls and asked for mercy. Then Allah ordered all of them to get out of the garden and go down to the earth. Allah bestowed clothing on Adam and Eve to cover their shame. (Q. 2:34-36, 7:11-26)

There are two accounts of why Satan was expelled from the garden. The first was for causing Adam to slip from his estate (Q. 2:36), the second for refusing to worship Adam (Q. 7:12-13). When Satan saw that he was expelled from the garden, in anger he spitefully said to Allah that he would besiege man from every direction and told Allah that he would find man ungrateful. Allah said he would fill hell with all those who followed Satan (Q. 7:16-18). Allah said that he was going to make man and Satan enemies of one another. Adam learned words of inspiration from Allah and Allah turned to him in mercy. Allah said that whoever followed guidance from him (Allah) would have nothing to fear (Q. 2:37-38).

In the Bible

God made man in His own image[10], male and female, and gave him dominion over all living things: fish, birds, animals, and plants. Man was made from the dust of the ground and God breathed the breath of life into him and he became a living creature. The Lord placed the man in the Garden of Eden. Among all the varieties of trees in the garden there were two of great significance: the one in the middle of the garden was called the Tree of Life; another was called the Tree of the Knowledge of Good and Evil. Four rivers flowed out of the garden, including the two we know today as the Tigris and the Euphrates. God gave the man permission to eat the fruit of the trees of the garden with one exception: He was not to eat of the Tree of the Knowledge of Good and Evil, for if he would eat from that tree he would die. God gave Adam the responsibility to name all the creatures that were brought before him. But no helpmate existed for Adam. So, the Lord caused a deep sleep to fall on Adam and, while he was asleep, He took one of Adam's ribs and from it He formed woman. When Adam saw her and understood what God had done,

---

[10] Please see "Jesus: Restoring God's Image in Humans"

he said, "This at last is bone of my bones and flesh of my flesh; she shall be Woman, because she was taken out of Man" (Genesis 2:8-23, O.T.).

And then the Scripture adds: "Therefore a man shall leave his father and mother and hold fast to his wife, and they shall become one flesh. And the man and his wife were both naked and were not ashamed" (Genesis 2:24-25, O.T.).

Next comes an astonishing scene. With no explanation, we read that there was a talking, crafty serpent in the garden who spoke to the woman.[11] He began to sow doubt in her mind as to what God really said and suggested that if she ate of the Tree of the Knowledge of Good and Evil that she would not die, but that her eyes would be opened, and she would be like God. Seeing that the fruit of the tree was desirable and that it would give her wisdom, she took it, ate it, and gave some to her husband (Genesis 3:1-6, O.T.).

As soon as they had eaten this forbidden fruit, their eyes were opened, and they became aware that they were naked. So, they sewed fig leaves together to cover their nakedness. When they heard the voice of the Lord God while He was walking in the garden in the cool of the day, they hid themselves from His presence among the trees of the garden. When God called out to them, Adam said, "When I heard Your voice, I was afraid because I was naked, so I hid myself." And God asked, "Who told you that you were naked? Have you eaten from the forbidden tree?" Adam explained that his wife gave him the fruit to eat. Then the Lord turned to the woman and asked her

---

[11] In order to understand where the serpent came from and what his nature is like, please read the chapter on Satan.

what she had done. Her answer was straightforward: "The serpent deceived me and I ate." Next, the Lord spoke to the serpent, and He cursed the serpent and said that He would put enmity (hostile opposition) between him and the woman, and between his offspring and hers, and He made this prophecy: "He [the man] shall bruise your head and you shall bruise his heel" (Genesis 3:7-15, O.T.).

Then the Lord spoke to the woman and said that she would now have pain in childbearing and that her husband would rule over her. To the man He said that because of his disobedience the ground would be cursed with thorns and thistles, that he would eat his food from what he earned by the sweat of his face, and that he would return to the dust of the earth from which he was made (Genesis 3:16-19, O.T.).

Adam called his wife by the name Eve since she would be the mother of all living human beings. Then the Lord God made garments of skins for Adam and Eve and clothed them. The Lord sent them out of the garden, to prevent them from eating of the Tree of Life and therefore, live forever in their fallen, sinful state. From then on man, instead of living in the garden, now had to earn his bread by hard labor. Then the Lord put cherubim[12] and a flaming sword to guard the way back into the garden where the Tree of Life stood (Genesis 3:20-24, O.T.).

Commentary

It is obvious that the Quranic version is a variant of the

---

[12] A type of angel.

original Biblical account with some apparent differences. For example, at the time the Quran was written, Christians were talking about the "fall" of Adam, meaning his fall from his sinless state. Some commentators on the Quran interpreted "the fall" to mean a literal "fall" from the garden above the earth. Also, in the Biblical account there are concrete references to the geographical location of where the garden of Eden was in connection with two famous rivers that are still flowing in Iraq today, the Tigris and the Euphrates; in the Quranic retelling, there are no geographical details. As interesting as these observations are, there is something far more important.

In the Biblical account, God covered Adam and Eve with the skins of animals. This suggests the shedding of blood, the killing of those animals that were sacrificed to provide the animal-skin clothes to cover these two naked and shame-laden sinners. Here, in the foundational story of the beginning of humankind, as recorded in these inspired Scriptures, we are beginning to see the principle that God laid down: that there will be sacrifices required for the atoning of man's sins. The original meaning of "atonement" is to cover (their shame or their sin). Thus, in the very beginning of humankind, we see that God taught the idea of the shedding of sacrificial blood as an atonement for sin.

What you should notice, as we examine these ancient stories, is the recurring theme in all the lives of the prophets common to the Bible and the Quran—they always made blood sacrifices for the covering of their sins. As we now move on to the next chapter, we discover just how devastating Adam's sin would be, with history's first recorded murder.

Chapter 7

Cain and Abel

When Adam and Eve sinned, and were removed from the Garden of Eden, a difficult life followed. Heartbreak, pain, anger, murder—all of these came into being quickly with the birth of their first children.

In the Quran

This is the story that was recited about Adam's two sons (Q. 5:27-31): Both sons presented sacrifices to Allah. It was accepted from one but not the other. The one whose sacrifice was not accepted said to his brother, "I am going to kill you." His brother said, "Allah accepts the sacrifice of those who are righteous. If you lift your hand to kill me, I will not lift my hand to kill you. I fear Allah, the Sustainer of the world. I will let you do this, and you will be responsible for my sins as well as yours. And your lot will be with those in hellfire. This is the punishment for those who do wrong."

The hatred of the brother whose sacrifice was not accepted led him to kill his brother, whose body he left exposed on the ground. Allah sent a raven to scratch the ground to show this murderer how to bury his brother. In shame this brother said, "Woe is me. I was not as noble as this raven to know enough to bury the shame of my brother." Then he was filled with regrets.

In the Bible

In Genesis 4:1-16 (O.T.) we read that Adam's wife, Eve, conceived a son and named him Cain. She said, "I have gotten a man with the help of the Lord."[13] Apparently Eve thought she had gotten that son who would crush the head of Satan. Next. she gave birth to another son named Abel. Cain became a farmer and Abel became a shepherd.

Both sons brought offerings to the Lord, each according to their profession: Cain brought vegetables and Abel brought the firstborn of his flock and of their fat portions. The Lord valued the offering of Abel, but not the offering of Cain, whose heart was not right before God.

When Cain realized his offering was not acceptable, he became very angry. God spoke to Cain and said, "If you do well, you will be accepted, and if you do not do well, sin in you is trying to master you, but you must not let it."

When the two brothers were out in a field, Cain murdered his brother. The Lord spoke to Cain again and asked him where his brother was. Cain answered that he did not know and then asked, "Am I my brother's keeper?"

---

[13] The Hebrew word, "Cain," signifies "gotten."

The Lord asked, "What have you done? Your brother's blood is crying to Me from the ground (for justice). Now you are cursed from the ground which received your brother's blood from your hand. From now on the ground will not yield its fruit to you and you will be a fugitive and wanderer on the earth."

Cain protested and said, "This punishment is unbearable. Now You have removed me from this ground and I shall be hidden from Your face. Whoever finds me will kill me." In reply the Lord put a mark on Cain so that no one would attack him. Then Cain left the presence of the Lord and settled in the land east of Eden.

Commentary

Let's look at some of the highlights of the story in the Old Testament. Eve certainly must have been remembering God's prophecy that her son would crush Satan's head and may have presumed that Cain would be the son who would do that (Genesis 3:15). Her joy must have turned to excruciating horror when she realized that her first child turned out to be the murderer of her second son. When God sentenced Cain to be a fugitive for the rest of his life, she ended up losing both of her sons. What numbing pain she must have felt as it dawned on her that this was the consequence of her sin in listening to Satan, instead of obeying God back in the garden.

Now let's examine the heart of the story—the nature of the offerings that each brother brought to God and the attitude in which they were given. Abel brought the firstborn of his flock (presumably sheep) and portions of their fat. It is possible that this early in human history, he learned to burn this on an altar with fire. The burning fat would thus generate a fragrant odor. By doing this, Abel was revealing his understanding of God and His greatness. He chose to bring the firstborn of his flock to God who gave this flock to Abel in the first place. Abel also learned a lesson from how God treated his mother and father regarding their sin and shame. God Himself killed sacrificial animals to make clothes of the skins. These skins covered their shame and guilt. Abel learned this principle from his mother and father. The shed blood of the sacrifices symbolically covered or atoned for their sins. So, Abel's sacrifice was pleasing to God and, consequently, he was considered righteous in God's sight.

A study of Cain's character reveals a different story. God said that sin was "crouching at his door," seeking to dominate him. And it did. The Bible does not openly name this sin, but Cain's subsequent actions reveal that it was hatred of his brother and, ultimately, hatred of the righteousness that characterized his brother's character. With his mind darkened by this hatred, he did not recognize the fundamental principles that his brother had learned from the Lord's treatment of his parents' sin. It never occurred to Cain that vegetables would never symbolically be able to atone for sins. In fact, Cain in his spiritual blindness was not aware of his sin; God had to point it out. So, Cain chose an inappropriate offering— vegetables—as his rebellious gift to God. Neither he nor his offering was accepted by God. Hatred was described by Jesus Christ (*Isa al Masih*) as being the same as murder (Matthew 5:21-26, N.T.), and in this case of the tragedy in the first family mentioned in the Bible, that is exactly what happened.

Of the several lessons that could be gleaned from this narrative, the most important one is that it is blood that atones for sins: the blood of sacrificial animals, the firstborn of the flocks. God taught from the beginning that sacrificial blood would be an appropriate atonement.

When we examine the Quranic re-telling of the same story, we notice it is much briefer, only a third of the length of the original Bible story. We also notice that there is no mention of what each of the brothers offered to the Lord. Thus, the central reason for why one offering was accepted and not the other is omitted in the Quran. This is why it is important to consult the Bible to learn the deep spiritual truths that are contained in these stories. It is blood that atones for sin.

In the original story of Cain and Abel, we also notice that the martyred brother's blood cries out to God from the ground. In other words, the martyred man's life is calling for justice. Scripture teaches us that life is sacred because we are created in the image of God[14] (Genesis 9:6, O.T.). By the gift of spiritual discernment given to Abel, he understood this great principle with God. It is the blood that is given as an atonement for sin. Remember the word "atonement" meanings "covering." Implied in this word is the idea of covering a sinner's shame and guilt.

The Old Testament is about law and justice. It calls for vengeance and punishment for sins committed against God and man. But God provided the sacrificial system as

---

[14] See chapter "Jesus: Restoring God's Image in Humans."

the basis for hope for forgiveness. This will be increasingly clear as we proceed through these stories.

Chapter 8

Noah

As we get into this comparative study, it is important to keep in mind that the style of the Quran and the Bible are quite different. In the Bible the story of Noah is treated as one continuous narrative as found in Genesis 5:28 through 9:17 (O.T.). In the Quran, the material on Noah is used as an exhortation to warn the readers or hearers of the Quran to learn lessons from the story of Noah. The material on Noah is found in over thirty chapters of the Quran. No one single passage provides the full narrative.

In the Quran

Based on Q. 11:25-48, Allah sent Noah to deliver a clear warning to his generation. His message was, "Serve Allah or a grievous thing will happen to you." The people said to Noah, "You are nobody special: you are just like us." Noah replied that he had a clear sign (referring to the coming flood) and Allah had sent mercy to him (referring to the ark). The people replied, "You talk a lot, now show us what you have threatened." Noah replied that Allah would bring what he promised. and they would not be able to frustrate it. Noah was also accused of forging the message. So, Allah said to Noah not to grieve over the people because they are not going to believe.

Then Allah instructed Noah to build the ark, as the people were going to be overwhelmed by a flood. The people ridiculed Noah as he was building the ark. Allah said that the coming chastisement would cover the people with shame (that is to say, they would be drowned).

Then Allah commanded the fountains of the earth to gush forth. Allah told Noah to gather male and female animals of every sort. He said that only a few people would believe. One of Noah's sons refused to enter the ark and was drowned. Allah told Noah not to grieve over the son that drowned. The ark floated over the mountains.

When Allah commanded the waters to recede, the ark came to rest on Mount Judi. Then Allah commanded Noah to come down from the ark and exhorted him to persevere in righteousness.

This is the main story. There are other issues that are mentioned about Noah in various places in the Quran.[15] Noah told people to submit to Allah. This is often repeated in the various verses about Noah. He was also accused of being possessed. Allah told Noah not to pray for non-believers. Noah was an apostle sent to warn people. Noah's wife was a non-believer and was destined for the fire. Noah prayed that Allah would not leave a single non-believer on the earth. Noah prayed that Allah would forgive his parents.

---

[15] See the end of this chapter for more Quranic references.

In the Bible

The Scriptures that present the record of Noah are located in the book of Genesis, chapters 6-9 (O.T.). Below is a summary of that story.

As a result of the unholy union of the godly with the godless in early human history, wickedness began to grow to the point where the thoughts and intentions of people's hearts were continually evil. The Lord was grieved in His heart and decided to blot men out. But there was one man and his family who found favor with the Lord. His name was Noah. He walked with God in righteousness and was blameless in His eyes. He lived in a world filled with violence. To save this godly family while judging the rest of mankind, the Lord instructed Noah to build an ark (a huge boat). It would be 450 feet long, 75 feet wide and 45 feet high. It was to have three levels or floors inside. It would have an entrance and a roof.

Then the Lord decreed that there would be a flood that would cover the world and destroy all living creatures on the earth. He gave further instructions to bring a male and female of every living species that breathed the air of the earth to be brought into the ark. God's plan was to repopulate the world with these animals, birds, and things that crept on the earth.

In addition to the male and female of every species, the Lord instructed Noah to bring into the ark seven pairs of "clean" animals and birds. (It was understood that these would be for burnt offerings after the flood.)

Before the flood came, Noah and his wife and Noah's three sons, Shem, Ham, and Japheth, and their wives entered the ark and the Lord shut them in. Noah was six hundred years old when the flood came.

There were forty days and nights of rain. In addition, the underground waters were released on the face of the earth. The flood rose and covered the tops of the mountains with twenty-two and a half feet of water. These waters prevailed on the earth for 150 days. At the end of this time, the waters began to recede, and the ark came to rest on Mount Ararat. The waters continued to recede for forty more days until the earth became dry. As soon as the earth became dry, Noah and his family came out of the ark and led all the animals and birds and all creeping things out.

The first thing that Noah did after he came out on dry ground was to build an altar to the Lord. There he offered some of the "clean" animals and birds as a burnt offering to the Lord. The aroma of these burnt offerings was very pleasing to the Lord. And the Lord said in His heart, "I will never again curse the ground because of man, even though the intention of man's heart is evil from his youth."

God blessed Noah and his sons and told them to be fruitful and multiply and fill the earth. He gave them every green plant and every moving thing as food. But there was one important prohibition. Man was not to eat the flesh of animals with the life (blood) in it.

God said he would require a reckoning for man's lifeblood, whether a man's blood was shed by an animal or his fellow man. Then He declared, "Whoever sheds the blood of man, by man shall his blood be shed, for God made man in His own image"[16] (Genesis 9:6, O.T.).

Then the Lord established his covenant with Noah and all humankind. He said that never again would all life on earth be destroyed by a worldwide flood. He gave the rainbow in the sky as sign of His covenant to all living creatures: "And God said, 'This is the sign of the covenant that I have established between Me and you and every living creature that is with you on the earth...'" (Genesis 9:12, O.T.). Then speaking of Noah's three sons, Shem, Ham and Japheth, God said, "From these the people of the whole earth were dispersed."

Commentary

As you compare the summary of the accounts in the Bible and in the Quran, you will find various differences. This is because the ancient account found in the Bible was written two thousand years before the Quran was written down. There was no Bible in the Arabic language before the birth of Islam. Knowledge was received by word of mouth.

After saving one family from the judgment of the flood, God chose to begin a new relationship with humankind through the calling of Abraham to a new land.

---

[16] See chapter "Jesus: Restoring God's Image in Humans."

Additional Quranic references on Noah:

Q. 3:33; 4:163; 6:84; 7:59, 69; 9:70; 10:71; 11:25-48, 89; 14:9; 17:3, 17, 19, 58; 21:76; 22:42; 23:23-30; 25:37; 26:105-119, 116; 29:14; 33:7; 37:75-82; 38:12; 40:5, 31; 42:13; 50:12; 51:46; 53:52; 54:9-14; 57:26; 69:11; 71:1-28

Chapter 9

Abraham

Muslims look to Abraham as the father of Islam. Jews look to Abraham as the father of their race. Christians look to Abraham as the father of faith.

Undoubtedly, Abraham is a very important person in history. That is why we must spend a considerable amount of time looking at what the Quran and the Bible have to say about this man.

In the Quran

Abraham (*Ibrahim*) is mentioned in twenty-eight chapters of the Quran.[17] Sometimes Abraham's name is simply mentioned in a list of other Quranic prophets.

Instead of one continuous narrative, as is found in the Biblical account, the Abrahamic story is broken up into scattered passages throughout the Quran and contains much repetition. In this study, only the material that is of some interest as agreeing with or contrasting with Biblical material are summarized as follows.

---

[17] All of the Quranic references are listed at the end of the chapter.

Abraham was tested by the Lord (no details as to how he was tested) and appointed as an imam to the people.[18] Abraham and Ismail built the foundation of a house and sanctified it. The "House" was to be a place of prayer. Abraham asked Allah to make him a Muslim and show him the rites of Islam. Abraham submitted to Allah and taught his sons to do the same. (Islam) takes its hue (like cloth is dipped in a dying vat) from Allah (Q. 2:124-140).[19]

Abraham asked Allah to show him how he would give life to the dead. There follows the story of Abraham cutting four birds into pieces and scattering the pieces on the hills; if they came back to life and returned to him, this would reassure Abraham that Allah would raise the dead (Q. 2:260).

Abraham argued with his father about his idolatry (repeated in several chapters). Allah showed Abraham the kingdom of heaven and earth (Q. 6:74-81).

Messengers (angels) came to Abraham, who prepared food for them. They revealed that their purpose was to bring chastisement on a sinful people. Only Lot (*Lut*) would be saved, but not his wife. This story is repeated several times in the Quran. In one of them the angels say Abraham's wife will have a child (Q. 11:69-83).

Abraham prays that his offspring will dwell near the House (*Kaaba*) for prayer. He thanks Allah for Ismail and Isaac and asks forgiveness for all the family (Q. 14:35-41).

---

[18] Please note: The word "imam" occurs nowhere in the Bible. It is introduced in the Quran as a word of its own day.

[19] Some think this is the Quranic way of referring to the dipping of baptism.

Abraham was a model of obedience; he was of the company of the righteous. Abraham did not add other "gods" to Allah (Q. 16:120-128).

Abraham appealed to his father not to follow the way of Satan. He prayed for his father to be forgiven. This is mentioned in several passages. Then later, Allah tells him not to pray for his father (Q. 19:41-50).

Abraham challenged his father's idols to speak. When they didn't speak, he broke them. Then Abraham was thrown into the fire but it did not burn him. Abraham established regular times of prayer and gave alms (*zakat*) (Q. 21:51-73).

Allah taught Abraham to walk around the House of Prayer. He established the pilgrimage (*Hajj*) and told him where *they were to sacrifice animals and eat the meat* (Q. 22:26-28, emphasis added).

No meat or blood reaches Allah; it is only one's piety that reaches Allah (Q. 22:37).[20]

Allah gave the Muslim people the religion of Abraham and named them "Muslims" (Q. 22:78).

Allah gave Abraham good news of a son to be born, though no name is given. Abraham dreamt he was to offer his son as a sacrifice. He shared the dream with his son, who offered himself as a willing sacrifice. At the last moment, Allah stopped Abraham from killing his son and

---

[20] This is in keeping with the Quranic teaching that there is nothing that can be given as an atonement for sin, Q. 10:54, Abdullah Yusuf Ali, *The Meaning of the Holy Quran*, second edition, 1977.

told him he had passed his test. Then a ram was offered as a sacrifice and Allah said, "And We *ransomed him with a momentous sacrifice*"[21] (Q. 37:107, emphasis added). Then Allah gave Abraham the good news of Isaac, a prophet, one of the righteous; Allah blessed Abraham and Isaac (Q. 37:100-113).

God established Islam as the religion of all the prophets. This began with Adam, and included Abraham, as well as David, Solomon, John the Baptist, and Jesus (Q. 42:13).

Abraham was an excellent example to follow (Q. 60:4).

The above is a summary of all the material in the Quran relevant to this study on Abraham. Note that there is much material included in the Quranic account that does not appear in the Biblical account.

In the Bible

The Biblical account begins with the genealogy of Abraham, progresses through his call, through all the major events of his life, and ends with the story of his death at the age of 175. This account is comprised of fourteen continuous chapters in the Old Testament, Genesis chapters 12 through 25.

Many generations after Noah, we read of the Lord appearing to Abraham. This would be approximately 2,100 years before the time of Christ. Since all three

---

[21] This is a unique passage in the Quran. In fact, this is the only passage to use the word "ransomed" in a "Biblical" sense. There is no explanation of what made it a "momentous" sacrifice.

monotheistic faiths (Islam, Christianity, and Judaism) trace their foundations back to Abraham, let's take a careful look at the significant events in the life of Abraham and particularly his "call":

> Now the Lord said to Abram[22], "Go from your country and your kindred and your father's house to the land that I will show you. And I will make of you a great nation, and I will bless you and make your name great, so that you will be a blessing. I will bless those who bless you, and him who dishonors you I will curse, and in you all the families of the earth shall be blessed."
> Genesis 12:1-3 (O.T.)

God promised Abram all the land of Canaan. Abram built an altar there by the great oak trees of Shechem (Genesis 12:7, O.T.).

Abram journeyed on, pitched his tent between Bethel and Ai, and built an altar there and worshiped the Lord (Genesis 12:8, O.T.).

Abram and his nephew, Lot, who traveled with him, eventually separated. Lot took the land around Sodom and Gomorrah. Abram was left with the rest of the land of Canaan, that is, from the river of Egypt to the Euphrates River, and included land on the east side of the Jordan River, as well as to the west side all the way to the coast of the Mediterranean Sea (Genesis 13:8-13, O.T.).

---

[22] Please note that at the beginning of the Biblical account, he is initially called "Abram," though the Lord changed his name later to "Abraham." This is not a typographical error.

Abram went to live in Hebron and built an altar there (Genesis 13:18, O.T.).

Abram rescued Lot, who was taken captive, and brought him back. After his great victory, Abram was met by Melchizedek, King of Salem (Jerusalem), a priest of God. Melchizedek's title is made up of two Hebrew words: *melek*, meaning "king," and *tsedek*, which means "righteousness." Thus, his name means the King of Righteousness. This is the king and priest who brought bread and wine and blessed Abram[23] (Genesis 14, O.T.).

God appeared to Abram and told him that a seed of his line would fulfill this prophecy of blessing to all mankind. But since Abram had no children, he complained to the Lord that he had no seed. So God took Abram outside that night and asked him to look at all the stars of heaven and said, "So shall your offspring be." Abram believed God and it was counted to him as righteousness (Genesis 15, O.T.).

Then Abram asked God for confirmation of this promise of many descendants and the possession of the land of Canaan. God instructed Abram to bring the traditional three kinds of animals and two kinds of birds to confirm this Covenant. Abram prepared the animals for this great event. He killed the animals, cleaned them and cut them in half with a space between the halves, and also put a bird on either side.[24] Then God manifested His presence with a

---

[23] Later in Psalm 110:4b (O.T.), and then in the book of Hebrews 5:6 (N.T.), we learn that Jesus is a "priest forever after the order of Melchizedek." Significantly, Jesus followed this example of Melchizedek and used "bread and wine" to inaugurate the New Covenant which is also known today as "the Lord's Supper" (Matthew 26:26-28, N.T.).

[24] Some scholars think this was the way ordinary men made a covenant of friendship

smoking pot and a flaming torch. God, with this smoking pot and torch of fire, moved between the cut pieces of the sacrifices and prophesied things of the future. Abram was in a deep trance when God made this covenant. God also prophesied that Abram's descendants would be slaves in a foreign land (Egypt) for 400 years (Genesis 15:8-21, O.T.).

The story of Abram's wife, Sarai[25], who thought she would be barren for the rest of her life, gave Hagar, her Egyptian slave girl, to her husband to bear a child. Hagar gave birth to Ishmael when Abram was eighty-six years old (Genesis 16, O.T.).

Later, God appeared to Abram when he was ninety-nine years old and gave the covenant rite of circumcision for all males, and also at the same time promised that Sarai, aged eighty-nine years old, was going to have a child named Isaac a year later. The name "Isaac" meant "laughter," because Sarah laughed when God said she would bear a child in her old age. At this time, God also gave Abram[26] a new name, Abraham, saying, "for I have made you the father of a multitude of nations." He also renamed Sarai as Sarah, "…she will become nations; kings of peoples shall come from her" (Genesis 17, O.T.).

Abraham received a visit from three heavenly visitors, one of them the Lord, announcing that He intended to destroy the cities of Sodom and Gomorrah, the home of Lot and his family. Abraham interceded for Sodom and Gomorrah.

---

to one another. Some also think that from this time forward Abram was called "The Friend of God." See 2 Chronicles 20:7 and Isaiah 41:8 in the Old Testament and James 2:23 in the New Testament where Abraham is called "the Friend of God").
[25] Later renamed Sarah.
[26] Abram meant "exalted father."

But Sodom and Gomorrah were destroyed. Lot and his two daughters are rescued by the two angels, but Lot's wife disobeyed the Lord and was turned into a pillar of salt (Genesis 18 and 19, O.T.).

After the birth of Isaac, about two years later, at his weaning celebration, Ishmael mocked Isaac. Sarah was outraged at this insult to her son and insisted that Hagar and Ishmael be discharged from their service. Abraham gave them their freedom (they were slaves), provisioned them and sent them away (Genesis 21, O.T.).

God tested Abraham by ordering him to sacrifice his son, Isaac, as a test of absolute loyalty to God. Abraham and Isaac made a three-day journey to Mount Moriah (later the site of Jerusalem). Abraham built an altar and put firewood on it. Isaac asked his father about a lamb for the burnt offering. "Abraham said, 'God will provide for Himself the lamb for a burnt offering, my son'" (Genesis 22:8). Then Abraham bound his son. At the very moment when Abraham was about to kill him, an angel of the Lord stopped Abraham. The Lord said, "Now I know that you fear God, seeing you have not withheld from Me your son, your only son" (Genesis 22:12b). God provided a ram as a substitute for the sacrifice of Isaac. And God said that it would be through Isaac's descendants that the promised seed would come and through this seed His promise would be fulfilled.

Commentary

As interesting as it might be to compare these two accounts detail by detail (and the reader can do so at his or her leisure), what we are looking for is the material that has to do with sacrifices and burnt offerings for sins. In the summary of the Biblical account above, we noted that on three significant occasions Abraham built an altar and offered burnt sacrifices on these altars. Each time Abraham set up a major campsite, he built an altar there and sacrificed a burnt offering for sin (Genesis 12:7; 12:8; and 13:18, O.T.).[27] Later, we see that Isaac carried on this tradition of his father, Abraham (Genesis 26:25, O.T.), as did Jacob, Isaac's son, after him (Genesis 31:54; 33:20, O.T.). The third time that Jacob built an altar was at the historic city of Bethel[28], and it is here that God spoke directly to Jacob, instructing him to make an altar: "Arise, go up to Bethel and dwell there. Make an altar there to the God who appeared to you when you fled from your brother Esau" (Genesis 35:1, O.T.). Then Jacob said to his household, "[T]hen let us arise and go up to Bethel, so that I may make an altar to the God who answers me in the day of my distress and has been with me wherever I have gone" (Genesis 35:3, O.T.).

Throughout the Bible, God identifies Himself as "the God of Abraham, Isaac and Jacob."[29] Jesus Himself, in addressing the question of the resurrection, said, "And as for the resurrection of the dead, have you not read what was said to you by God: 'I am the God of Abraham, and the God of Isaac, and the God of Jacob'? He is not God of the dead, but of the living" (Matthew 22:31-32, N.T.).

In the family of Abraham and Isaac, we assume that they learned from the living tradition of their predecessors,

---

[27] Please see the footnote in Chapter 4 linking the terms "altar" with "sacrifice."

[28] Beth-El means the "House of God."

[29] See, for example, Exodus 3:6 and Exodus 4:5 in the O.T.

including Noah, that blood sacrifices were required when man approached God—the blood of the sacrifice that atoned for the sin of the worshiper. In the case of Jacob, we read that God Himself explicitly directed Jacob to build an altar at Bethel and offer sacrifices there. So, we see that it is not only oral traditions handed down from generation to generation, but the Lord Himself mandated this.

We need to remember that God changed Abram's name from "Exalted Father" to Abraham, which means "the Father of Many Nations" (Genesis 17:5, O.T.). Later, in the New Testament, the Apostle Paul refers back to this event, and in his words, writes, "...to the one who shares the faith of Abraham, who is father of us all" (Romans 4:16, N.T.). This calls for an explanation: In Genesis 15 (O.T.), we read the story of God taking Abraham at night and commanding him to look at the stars and number them if he could, and said, "So shall your offspring be" (Genesis 15:5, O.T.). Abraham *believed* God and it was counted (that is, credited) to him as *righteousness*. This illustrates the principle of believing or trusting God, or having faith in God, and then being found righteous in God's eyes. From this is derived the principle of "justification by faith." This implies that we can only be saved, not by our own effort, but by what God has done for us, if we believe.

Jews, Christians, and Muslims all claim Abraham as the "Father of their faith." This being so, it is therefore very important that we have the same kind of faith that Abraham did. If we follow Abraham's example, then we, too, are saved by the same kind of faith or trust he had in God's provision. Here it would mean adhering to the teaching and example of offering sacrifices for sin whenever we approach God. This was exemplified in the life of all three patriarchs, Abraham, Isaac and Jacob, and especially in the example of Jacob when God spoke to him directly to build an altar at Bethel and offer sacrifices there. This leads us to believe that this requirement of a sacrifice must be highly significant in God's unfolding plan for the salvation of humans.

Notice how this promise of God's to make Abraham's name great has been fulfilled. Today all 1.7 billion Muslims honor his name; all 16 million Jews honor his name; and all 2.3 billion Christians honor his name. This is over half of the world's population. And those non-monotheists who live near Muslims, Jews and Christians often hear his name. What a fulfillment of prophecy! God made Abraham great because he believed in God.

There is so much more in the above passage to ponder. Abraham was uprooted from the land of his birth, the Chaldean city of Ur, and was commanded to go to a land God would show him. In other words, God asked Abraham to trust Him to be led to a land he had never seen. Of course, we read later in Scripture that Abraham obeyed. He walked with God by faith.

Another point worth noting is the emphasis on the word "blessing." In a world under the curse of God (see Genesis 3:17, O.T.), this word "blessing" is a huge word. It leaps out at you. In a world of floods, earthquakes, ice storms, heat waves, hurricanes, tornadoes, famines, diseases, wars, and death, this word "blessing" is the answer to every hungering heart. Not only was Abraham blessed by God, but much more, he and his offspring were to be the agents of blessing to all the families of the earth. That idea is worth pondering. How will God work this out? As the Bible unfolds through time, we shall see God's most unexpected way of fulfilling this promise.

In the next chapter we will see how dramatically God's sacrifice was institutionalized in the rituals of the Hebrew nation.

Additional Quranic references on Abraham:

Q. 2:124-140; 2:258-260; 3:33; 3:65-68, 84; 4:125, 163; 6:74-84, 161; 9:114; 11:69-76; 12:6, 38; 14:35-41; 15:51-60; 16:120-123; 19:41-58; 21:51-72; 22:78; 26:69-104; 29:16-32; 33:7; 37:83-109; 38:45; 42:13; 43:26; 51:24-34; 53:37; 57:26; 60:4; 87:19.

Chapter 10

Moses

In following the line of Abraham, we find in both the Quran and the Bible that Abraham was the father of Isaac, who in turn was the father of Jacob (also known as "Israel" after the Lord changed his name; see Genesis 32:28, O.T., for more details), who in turn was the father of the twelve patriarchs or tribes. Both books give an account of how the ten older brothers envied Jacob's/Israel's special affection for Joseph (*Yusuf*). Both accounts speak of Joseph being taken by traders to Egypt and made a slave in a certain household; how he gained the trust of the head of the house but was tempted by the wife; and how when he fled, she grasped an article of his clothing and showed it to her husband, who had Joseph cast into prison.

Through a series of circumstances, Joseph was able to interpret the dreams of Pharaoh, who then released him from prison and made him second in command of the entire country. A desperate famine brought Joseph's brothers to Egypt for food and eventually their entire family settled in Egypt (Q. 12:4-101; Genesis 37:1-47:28, O.T.).

As time passed, old Pharaohs died and new Pharaohs arose, and Joseph's deeds were forgotten. The Egyptians became concerned by the fertility and robustness of the Hebrew people, so they enslaved the Hebrews for hundreds of years. This is where we pick up the story of Moses.

In the Quran

This material has been rearranged chronologically, as fragments of the story of Moses are found in twenty-four chapters in the Quran and are not presented as a linear narrative.[30]

Moses was born under abnormal circumstances when Pharaoh ordered all newborn Hebrew baby boys to be cast into the Nile River to be drowned. Moses was rescued by Pharaoh's wife and was then nursed by his own mother. As an adult, when he saw an Egyptian man fighting with a Hebrew, he intervened and killed the Egyptian. He then had to flee for his life to the land of Midian, where he married the local chief's daughter.

One day, while tending his father-in-law's flocks in a green valley, he saw a burning bush that was not consumed by the fire. Through it, Allah spoke to Moses and commanded him to go back to Egypt and confront a proud and evil Pharaoh who was grievously oppressing the

---

[30] Here are the main references in the Quran about Moses: 2:51-61; 5:22-26; 7:103-157; 10:75-92; 17:101-103; 20:9-97; 23:49; 28:3-4; 28:15-48; 40:36; 43:46-56. There are over 400 verses in the Quran about Moses. Much of the material is repeated many times.

Hebrew people. Moses claimed to be slow of speech, so Allah appointed his brother, Aaron, to be his spokesman.

In Pharaoh's court, Moses showed two supernatural signs: first, he cast his staff on the ground, which became a snake and consumed the staffs/snakes of the local magicians; then he put his hand within his cloak, drew it out and displayed it as being affected by a skin disease, then put his hand in his cloak again and showed that it came out completely normal.

Pharaoh was not impressed and denied Moses' request to let the Hebrew people go into the desert to worship the true God. Then began a series of nine plagues that progressively destroyed the land of Egypt.

Finally, in desperation, Pharaoh decided to let the Hebrews go. By now the Egyptian people were in fear of the Hebrews. The Egyptians gave away all of their expensive jewelry to the Hebrews.

The Hebrews set out from Egypt. Subsequently, Pharaoh changed his mind and sent his army to capture the Hebrews and bring them back. Moses prayed for Allah to part the sea so they could cross on dry ground. The Hebrews crossed on dry land. But when Pharaoh's army followed them, the sea covered the army and they all drowned.

The Hebrews had no more food, and they complained to Moses. He prayed to Allah, and Allah sent "manna" and quail from heaven. Later, as they traveled into the wilderness, they became thirsty and again complained to

Moses. Allah told him to strike a rock and twelve springs of water came out, one for each of the tribes.

Eventually, the Hebrews arrived at Mount Tur (Sinai). Allah called Moses up to Mount Tur for forty days and nights. During that time, Allah gave him the revelation of the Book and the tablets on which the covenant was written. While Moses was on the side of the mountain, the Hebrew people turned away from Allah and appealed to Moses' brother to make a cow-idol as their god. When Moses came down from the mountain, he was furious with his brother Aaron and pulled his hair and rebuked him. The people who did this were punished with a plague.

After this the Hebrews were supposed to go to the Promised Land that Allah had promised to Abraham. Seventy elders were appointed. Allah punished the Sabbath-breakers (Hebrews) by turning them into apes. The Hebrews rebelled against Allah, except for two men. Allah punished them by causing them to wander in distress for forty years.

There is a gap of approximately 2,000 years between the original account in the Bible and the partial retelling of the story of Moses in the Quran. The amount of material written about or by Moses is contained in four of the five books of the Torah (the first five books of the Old Testament), in 137 chapters, totaling at least 2,800 verses. The Quran touches on only a small fraction of the Biblical material on Moses. In fact, no more than fourteen percent of the Biblical material on Moses is touched on in the Quran. What is intriguing in this study are the two most important events in the remaining eighty-six percent of the

Biblical material that is unmentioned in the Quran: (1) the tenth plague in Egypt and (2) what happened between God and Moses on the mountain in the Sinai wilderness.

In the Bible

The Bible and the Quran cover much of the same material on the birth of Moses, his flight to Midian, his return to Egypt, and his dramatic confrontations with Pharaoh. Let's take up the story in the Bible with the nine plagues. They occurred in the following order: (1) the Nile River turned to blood, (2) the plague of frogs, (3) the plague of gnats, (4) the plague of flies, (5) the plague on livestock, (6) the plague of boils, (7) the plague of hail, (8) the plague of locusts, and (9) the plague of darkness. After each plague, God hardened Pharaoh's heart. Pharaoh was not going to let the Hebrew people go free after 400 years of slavery in Egypt. This led to the tenth plague (not mentioned in the Quran). Let's read about this tenth plague:

> The Lord said to Moses, "Yet one plague more I will bring upon Pharaoh and upon Egypt. Afterward he will let you go from here."
> Exodus 11:1 (O.T.)

> So Moses said, "Thus says the Lord: 'About midnight I will go out in the midst of Egypt, and every firstborn in the land of Egypt shall die, from the firstborn of Pharaoh who sits on his throne, even to the firstborn of the slave girl who is behind the hand mill, and all the firstborn of the cattle.'"
> Exodus 11:4-5 (O.T.)

The Lord said to Moses and Aaron in the land of Egypt, "This month shall be for you the beginning of months. It shall be the first month of the year for you. Tell all the congregation of Israel that on the tenth day of this month every man shall take a lamb according to their fathers' houses, a lamb for a household. And if the household is too small for a lamb, then he and his nearest neighbors shall take according to the number of persons...Your lamb shall be without blemish, a male a year old...You shall keep it until the fourteenth day of this month, when the whole assembly of the congregation of Israel shall kill their lambs at twilight. Then they shall take some of the blood and put it on the two doorposts and the lintel of the houses in which they eat it."
Exodus 12:1-7 (O.T.)

"...It is the Lord's Passover. For I will pass through the land of Egypt that night, and I will strike all the firstborn in the land of Egypt, both man and beast, and on all the gods of Egypt I will execute judgments: I am the Lord. The blood shall be a sign for you on the houses where you are. And when I see the blood, I will pass over you, and no plague will befall you to destroy you, when I strike the land of Egypt."
Exodus 12:11b-13 (O.T.)

"This day shall be for you a memorial day, and you shall keep it as a feast to the Lord; throughout your generations, as a statute forever, you shall keep it as a feast."

Exodus 12:14 (O.T.)

At midnight the Lord struck down all the firstborn in the land of Egypt, from the firstborn of Pharaoh who sat on his throne to the firstborn of the captive who is in the dungeon, and all the firstborn of the livestock.
Exodus 12:29 (O.T.)

And Pharaoh rose up in the night, he and all his servants and all the Egyptians. And there was a great cry in Egypt, for there was not a house where someone was not dead. Then he summoned Moses and Aaron by night and said, "Up, go out from among my people, both you and the people of Israel; and go, serve the Lord as you have said. Take your flocks and your herds, as you have said, and be gone, and bless me also!"
Exodus 12:30-32 (O.T.)

The Quran confirmed the first nine plagues that God performed through Moses against all the gods of Egypt. But it is silent concerning the last great judgment of God on Pharaoh, who claimed to be a god and on all the Egyptians who treated Pharaoh as a god.

This great deliverance of the Jewish people was so important in the eyes of the Lord that He wanted it to be memorialized for all generations. It was to be called the "Feast of the Passover." The word "Passover" refers to the fact that the Angel of Death passed over every house where he saw the blood of the sacrificial lamb smeared on the lintels and doorposts of the Hebrew houses. This was considered the greatest feast under the first covenant of

God with His people, for it celebrated their great deliverance from slavery in Egypt.

What is so interesting to those who read both the Quran and the Bible are the similarities and differences between the killing of a sacrificial animal in Islam (Q. 37:107, a mighty or momentous sacrifice) and among the Israelites (a one-year-old male lamb without any blemish in it) and the communal meal that followed. The difference is that in Islam, no significance is given to the blood of the "mighty sacrifice," whereas, in the Bible, the blood of the sacrificial lamb is extremely important. In fact, it was a matter of life or death for the Hebrews and Egyptians. If they put the blood on their doorposts and lintel, the Angel of Death would pass over them; if there was no blood on the doorposts and lintel, the firstborn of that household would die, even the firstborn of the animals.

From this story in the Bible, we discover the real reason the Egyptians let the people of Israel leave. Then as we read on in both the Quran and the Bible, we learn that Pharaoh changed his mind and pursued the Hebrews even into the midst of the dry land where God parted the waters of the Red Sea for the Hebrews but then brought the waters back over Pharaoh's army, drowning all of them. Be that as it may, the most important thing to remember as we follow this trail of blood through these early revealed accounts is an amazing continuity: The covering of sin is accomplished by the blood of sacrificial animals. In fact, it is a matter of life and death: life for those who believed and obeyed, and death for those who didn't.

Continuing on the theme of the trail of blood, we want to look into the awesome event of Moses' forty days with God, face to face on Mount Sinai, also called Mount Horeb in the Bible and Mount Tur in the Quran. What were the burning issues on God's heart that caused Him to call up Moses for forty days, not once, but twice, on that fiery mountain?

God was in process of laying out His plan to Moses, His plan of how to create a unique nation in the world that would be a true theocracy. At the heart of this plan was a worship center called the "Tent of Meeting." Remember, the Hebrew people were living in the wilderness and would be doing so for the next forty years. God's Presence would come down in a cloud of glory and Moses would meet Him in the Tent of Meeting. This Tent of Meeting (also called a tabernacle) was replaced centuries later, according to God's instruction, by an elaborate temple. This also required the appointment of priests to prepare the animals for the burnt offerings morning and evening at the Tent of Meeting and later in the Temple.

As the plan was explained to Moses by God during those forty days when Moses was at the top of the mountain with God, the plan required setting aside one of the twelve tribes, (Moses' own tribe), the Levites, to be priests of the Lord. Along with this were instructions for many kinds of sacrifices to be offered to God to atone for various offenses the people committed against the holy God. The priests were the ones who handled the sacrificial animals and their blood on behalf of the common people. These priests were to be consecrated for their holy duty before God by having blood sprinkled on their priestly garments.

God explained to Moses the key meaning of this elaborate sacrificial system: "For the life of the flesh is in the blood, and I have given it for you on the altar to make atonement for your souls, for it is the blood that makes atonement by the life" (Leviticus 17:11, O.T.).

This is a very brief summary of pages and pages of God's instruction to Moses and his brother Aaron on how to approach God in worship. Because of these sacrifices, the people could worship God without fear of judgment, and know that when they were truly repentant and offered these sacrifices to God with a true heart, they could be assured that their sins were forgiven.

We must notice that throughout the Bible, blood is a constant theme and is of great importance in God's eyes. Continuing on, we will see how God teaches us about the profound meaning of blood in spiritual matters.

Chapter 11

Job

It is apparent that Job (*Ayyub*) was a man of great wealth and tremendous influence. His trust in God was proven to be very strong. His integrity with God was solid. His patience in great affliction is an example for many. He is a man we need to know better.

In the Quran

Job is listed among those who received inspiration (Q. 4:163) and among those whom Allah guided (Q. 6:84)

Job cried to the Lord in distress. Allah removed the distress and doubled the number of his people (Q. 21:83-84). Job cried to Allah, "Satan has afflicted me with distress and suffering." Allah instructed Job to strike his foot (against a rock) and water would come out for drink and for washing himself. Allah gave back his people and doubled their number. Then Allah commanded him to strike[31] with a little grass. Job was patient and constant in turning to God (Q. 38:41-44).

---

[31] "… strike his wife," according to the Ali commentary.

When we consult the Bible, we discover many interesting details that clarify the circumstances, the location of where Job lived and what the purpose was of this story in the Bible.[32]

In the Bible

As we get into the account in the Biblical story, we discover that this is a very long record of what some have described as the greatest duel between a man and Satan in all of literature. In fact, this report is a "book" of the Old Testament (O.T.) in its own right named "Job."

It focuses on a godly man, a righteous man who was blameless in the eyes of God. The book ends with God blessing this man, to whom God gave a new family of seven sons and three daughters to replace those he lost. He gave him double of what he owned before the terrible devastation of all that he had at the hands of Satan.

With regard to the date of when Job lived, there are very few clues. The Hebrew language of the Old Testament book closely resembles ancient Arabic. He could have lived shortly after the period of Abraham, Isaac, and Jacob. He was known as the wealthiest man in the East, probably in northern Arabia. He owned 7,000 sheep, 3,000 camels, 500 yoke of oxen, and 500 female donkeys. Before God allowed Satan to test him, he had seven sons and three daughters.

---

[32] Remember that the Quran many times states that it confirms what the Bible says.

The drama began when Satan, in the presence of God, boasted that he had walked all over the world as though it all belonged to him. God asked him if he had considered Job, a man who was blameless in God's eyes. Satan said it was only because God protected him that Job served God. God gave Satan permission to afflict Job. Satan then destroyed Job's property, then his children, and then his health. That is when the great duel began between Satan and this godly man, Job.

As we get to the parts of Job's story that have to do with the main theme of this book, you might also be interested in some of the amazing things this man said as he was being tested by these afflictions that were caused by Satan. Of course, as the main theme of the book has to do with sacrificial offerings that were given to cover peoples' sins, those will be italicized in this text. (All material below is from the book of Job, unless otherwise indicated.)

> In the land of Uz there lived a man whose name was Job. This man was blameless and upright; he feared God and shunned evil.
> Job 1:1

Early in the morning *he would sacrifice a burnt offering for each of them* (his children), thinking, "Perhaps my children have sinned and cursed God in their hearts." This was Job's regular custom. We are told later that since their father was so wealthy, each of Job's seven sons often took turns in giving feasts to which his three daughters were invited (Job 1:5)[33].

---

[33] This and all the following references are from the book of Job in the Old Testament.

The Lord gave Satan permission to test Job. Satan killed Job's seven sons and three daughters, all of his herds of animals, most of his servants, and finally Satan afflicted Job with painful boils in his flesh (Job 1:12; 2:6-7).

Job said in response to these afflictions, "Naked I came from my mother's womb, and naked I will depart. The Lord gave and the Lord has taken away; blessed be the name of the Lord" (Job 1:21).

Job's three friends came to commiserate with him, sitting with him for seven days in silence (Job 2:11). Job finally spoke, saying, "For the thing that I fear comes upon me, and what I dread befalls me. I am not at ease, nor am I quiet; I have no rest, but trouble comes" (Job 3:25-26).

In Job chapters 4, 5, 8, and 11, Job's three friends begin to argue with him, saying that it is because of some hidden sin that all these calamities happened to him. Job replied to his friends' arguments, "Truly I know that it is so: But how can a man be in the right before God?"

All the while, Job reminded the Lord of all the righteous deeds he has done in caring for the poor, the widow, and orphans, etc. (Job 29:1-25). Job cried out, "There is no arbiter between us" (that is, between him and God). Job cried out for a mediator or an intercessor, that is, for someone to stand between him and God to bring justice and mercy (Job 9:33).

Job proclaimed, "Though He [God] slay me, I will hope in Him" (Job 13:15) and "Even now, behold, my witness is in heaven, and He who testifies for me is on High…[M]y eye pours out tears to God, that He would argue the case [as an intercessor or advocate] of the man with God, as a son of man does with his neighbor" (Job 16:19, 20b-21). This is amazing. Job here anticipates the coming of Jesus, who is described as this intercessor later in the Bible.

Job says further:

> "For I know that my Redeemer lives, and at the last He will stand upon the earth. And after my skin has been thus destroyed, yet in my flesh I shall see God, whom I shall see for myself, and my eyes shall behold, and not another. My heart faints within me" (Job 19:25-27).

Here the word "Redeemer" implies someone who will pay the price, in this case, in blood, to set someone free.

Job affirmed himself, saying "But He knows the way that I take; when He has tried me, I shall come out as gold" (Job 23:10). But he also complained bitterly of his situation in further chapters. He felt that God had not been fair with him. His three friends continually implied that Job had done something wrong to deserve such a fate. A younger man, who obviously had been a listener to the dialogue between Job and his three older friends, interrupted (Job chapter 25) and said, in essence, "What right does a sinful man have to argue with God?"

Finally, the Lord Himself intervened and recounts the wonders of His creation (Job chapters 38 through 41) and asks Job where he was and what did he really know about the greatness and the glory of God's unbelievably beautiful, intricate, and powerful creation.

Job became a humbled man, and following are some of his words: "…I have uttered what I did not understand, things too wonderful for me, which I did not know…I had heard of You by the hearing of the ear, but now my eye sees You; therefore I despise myself, and repent in dust and ashes" (Job 42:3b, 5-6).

Then the Lord rebuked Job's three friends for suggesting he had done that which he really had not done and commanded them in the following way:

> "Now therefore take seven bulls and seven rams and go to My servant Job and offer up a *burnt offering* for yourselves. And my servant Job will pray for you, for I will accept his prayer not to deal with you according to your folly" (Job 42:8, emphasis added).

Then the three friends did as the Lord commanded and the Lord accepted Job's prayer, "And the Lord restored the fortunes of Job, when he had prayed for his friends"; "And the Lord blessed the latter days of Job more than his beginning" (Job 42:10, 12). In blessing Job, it turned out to be double the number of animals that he had lost at the hands of Satan.

What we would like to call attention to is the emphasis on burnt offerings, that is, the slaying of animals, the shedding of their blood, to atone for sins. In the beginning of this Biblical book, sacrifices for the possible sins of Job's children are offered every time they had a feast. In the case of Job's three friends who spoke so foolishly, it was the shedding of the blood of the bulls and rams for their sins of presumption that atoned for their sins. Added to this was Job's intercessory prayer for the three friends who falsely accused him.

This is in keeping with God's initial kindness in covering Adam and Eve's shame, when he slaughtered animals, shed their blood, and made clothing from the skins of the slain animals for them. Their son Abel learned this lesson from what God did for his mother and father. Noah practiced this act of worship when he selected animals and birds specifically for sacrifice. Job offered sacrifices for his children's and his friends' sins. This lesson has been passed on from generation to generation. So, let's continue looking what happened next in this saga of human history.

Chapter 12

David

David was a very important man in history and to God. His exploits as a youth in killing a lion and a bear; in killing the giant, Goliath; and then his becoming a king, a prophet, and a writer of poetry and songs, all reveal that he was a diverse, gifted, and special man whom we need to know better.

In the Quran

The following summary about David (*Daud*) in the Quran is taken from twenty-one verses scattered across nine chapters. There is no record of his birth or long life of service. We shall list the comments about him as they occur in Q. 2, 4, 5, 6, 17, 21, 27, 34 and 38.[34]

- David slew Goliath.

- Allah gave him the psalms.

- Allah guided David.

---

[34] See Q. 2:250-51; 4:163; 5:78; 6:84; 17:55; 21:78-80; 27:15; 34:10-11, and 38:17-26.

- David cursed the Israelites who turned away from the faith. Allah gave good judgment in the case where a man's sheep strayed into his neighbor's field. He gave knowledge to David and taught David how to make chain-mail armor.

- The mountains and the birds gathered in unison and joined with David in praising Allah in the morning and the evening. David was a man of strength. Allah strengthened his kingdom. Two brothers climbed over a wall and got into David's private chamber to present their case to David. The one brother who owned one sheep complained against his brother who had ninety-nine sheep, who wanted to take his one sheep away from him. David said the rich brother was wrong. Allah tested David, who gave good judgment. Then David asked forgiveness from Allah, fell down and bowed and turned to Allah, who then forgave him. Allah made David a vicegerent[35] on earth, warned David not to follow lust, and reminded him that there is a day of accounting (judgment).

In the Bible

There are sixty-three chapters, comprising over 2,000 verses on the life of David, plus more than eighty psalms he composed under the inspiration of the Holy Spirit. The narrative describes how God chose him to be the King of Israel, the wars he went through, his conquests, his

---

[35] This is not a misspelling, just a very uncommon word with similar spelling to "vice-regent." It is a deputy appointed to act on the authority of a ruler or magistrate, especially in administrative duties.

recovery of the Ark[36] of the Covenant from the Philistines, his bringing the Ark of the Covenant to Jerusalem, his sin of committing adultery with Bathsheba, the rebellions in his court, and the installation of his son, Solomon, to succeed him.

There are three parts of David's story that concern us in this book. The first is his anointing to be the king of Israel by the prophet, Samuel. This is what we read in 1 Samuel 16:13a (O.T.), "Then Samuel took the horn of oil and anointed him [David] in the midst of his brothers. And the Spirit of God rushed upon David from that day forward."

This mention of the Spirit of God coming upon David from that day forward is very important. For we read from one end of the Bible to the other that all the prophets of God prophesied by the power of the Spirit of God. The Spirit of God, sometimes called "the Holy Spirit," is not a created being, but the actual, eternal Spirit of the Living God. It is this Spirit who empowers and guides the servants of God to do what the Lord really wants done. So, when we look at further events in the life of David, we need to remember that David is being inspired and moved by the Holy Spirit; not an angel, but the actual Spirit of God.[37]

Secondly, under David's predecessor, King Saul, there had been much war between the Israelites and the Philistines. In the war just before David was anointed king, the

---

[36] This word, "Ark" should not be confused with the ark of Noah's journey. While both are types of containers, one was an enormous boat built by Noah to save himself, his family, and the earth's creatures from the Great Flood. The other was a chest containing the Ten Commandments given to Moses by God, and other sacred objects.

[37] In Arabic and Hebrew the words are the same, "Ruh-ul-Quddus."

Philistines defeated Israel and captured what was called the Ark of the Covenant. This was a sacred religious item that was designed by God; Moses was the one who recruited craftsmen to make it. It was placed in the great Tent of Meeting, where the Lord would come down and commune with the High Priest, who led the worship for the people of Israel.

After the Philistines captured the Ark of the Covenant, they were afflicted with a fatal plague (1 Samuel chapters 5 and 6, O.T.). Wherever the Philistines kept the Ark, there people died from the plague. So the Philistines decided to return the Ark to the Israelites. It was David's privilege to recover the Ark. When he was in possession of it, after taking only a few steps on their way to Jerusalem, we read that David sacrificed an ox and a fattened animal (2 Samuel 6:1-15, O.T.). This was a sin offering for the sins of the people of Israel and to appease the wrath of God against all those who had disobeyed him. When David arrived in Jerusalem (which was called "the City of David" at that time), he placed the Ark in a tent he had prepared for it. Then David offered burnt offerings and peace offerings before the Lord there in Jerusalem.

Why were these offerings made at the beginning of the travel of the Ark to Jerusalem, and why were more offerings made again when the Ark came to its resting place? The answer is that God is a holy God. He cannot tolerate sin. Sin separates people from God. The people of Israel had sinned grievously against the Lord. These offerings were required by God as an atonement for the sins of the people.

Finally, one of the last activities in the life of David was to gather all the materials that would go into the building of a glorious Temple for the worship of God in Jerusalem. But God told David that because he was a man of war and had spilled much blood [of his enemies in battle], he would not be allowed to build that Temple. God said that David's son, Solomon, who would succeed him as king, was the one God chose to build the Temple (1 Chronicles 22:6-10, O.T.).

After David had collected all the gold and silver and brass and precious building materials, he set aside a special day to dedicate the material for the Lord's Temple. David caused burnt offerings to be offered to the Lord—1,000 bulls, 1,000 rams, and 1,000 lambs with their drink offerings—abundant sacrifices for all Israel. Literally, there were rivers of blood flowing from all of these sacrifices. So again, we ask the question, Why? Remember that this is all according to the Law of Moses. That Law required that these sacrifices be made as an atonement for the sins of the people: "For the life of the flesh is in the blood, and I [the Lord] have given it for you on the altar to make atonement for your souls, for it is the blood that makes atonement by the life [of the sacrificial animal]" (Leviticus 17:11, O.T.).

The theme of sacred blood shed for the sins of the people was greatly emphasized during the closing days of David's reign. But as we will discover in the next chapter, sacrifices take on a new scale of magnitude during the life of David's son, Solomon.

Chapter 13

Solomon

Historically, Solomon is considered to be one of the wisest and wealthiest people who ever lived upon this earth. Both the Quran and the Bible take special note of this man and the knowledge and discernment that he displayed before the people of his time.

In the Quran

The material about Solomon is found in five passages in the Quran: Q. 2:102; 4:163; 6:84; 21:78-82; and 27:15-44. We have taken the liberty of summarizing all of these passages referring to Solomon as follows:

The evil ones gave false information about the power of Solomon. The evil ones, not Solomon, taught magic from Babylon.

Solomon's name is above those to whom Allah gave inspiration. His name is among those who were guided by Allah.

Allah gave him (and David) good judgment in the matter of a man's sheep that wandered into his neighbor's field one night. Allah's power made the violent wind blow gently for Solomon. Allah gave special knowledge to Solomon (and David) above many others.

Allah taught Solomon the speech of the birds and many other things. Solomon gathered *Jinn* (spirits) and men in order and ranks. When they came to the valley of ants, one of the ants told the others to go into their habitations so as not to be trampled on by Solomon's host.

Solomon mustered all the birds and noticed that the Hoopoe (a bird) was missing. Solomon threatened to punish the Hoopoe unless he gave a good reason for his absence. The Hoopoe came and said he have traveled far and found a woman ruling over a kingdom called Saba (Sheba) with a magnificent throne. The queen and her people were worshiping the sun. Satan made it seem pleasing to them. But he (Satan) kept them from Allah, who is light in heaven and on earth.

Solomon said to the Hoopoe that he would see whether he was telling the truth or not. He told the Hoopoe to take a letter and see how they respond to it. The queen said that it was a worthy letter from Solomon. (In the letter) he said to be not arrogant, but to come to him (Solomon) in submission.

The queen took counsel from her chiefs. They said she should decide what to do. Solomon asked his chiefs, "Who can bring me her throne?" An *Ifrit* (evil spirit) of the *Jinn* said he would bring her throne. When she arrived at Solomon's court, she recognized her throne. Then Solomon converted the queen to believe in God. She was invited to Solomon's palace. She thought the pavement of glass was a lake of water. She lifted up her skirt and exposed her legs as if she was going to walk in the water. When she recognized her mistake, she then submitted to the Lord of the worlds with Solomon.

In the Bible with Commentary

Solomon was born 1,033 years before Christ. His father was the famous King David. His mother's name was Bathsheba. He died in the year 975 BC. He lived about 1,600 years before Muhammad. His story is told in nineteen chapters of the Old Testament in a total of 557 verses.

Under Solomon's rule, the borders of his kingdom stretched from the Euphrates River in modern day Iraq to Al Arish River in the Sinai Peninsula, bordering the territory of Egypt. Thus, the promise made to Abraham a thousand years earlier was finally fulfilled under Solomon. The glory of his kingdom was unrivalled.

Recall that God spoke to David about gathering all the materials that would be needed to build a glorious temple for the worship of God. Because David was a man of war who had shed lots of blood, God chose Solomon, David's son, a man of peace[38], to build God's Temple. This was to be a vast improvement over the Tent of Meeting of Moses. This was to be a glorious temple in Jerusalem. Let's see what Solomon had to say about building God's Temple; he announced his plan as follows:

---

[38] Solomon's name means "peace."

"Behold, I am about to build a house for the name of the Lord my God and dedicate it to Him for the burning of incense of sweet spices before Him, and for the regular arrangement of the showbread, and for the burnt offerings morning and evening, on the Sabbaths and the new moons and the appointed feasts of the Lord our God...The house that I am to build will be great, for our God is greater than all gods."
2 Chronicles 2:4-5 (O.T.)

The functions of these things were as follows:

- The sweet-smelling incense was to be offered at the time of the burnt offerings. It symbolized the prayers of the worshippers rising to God in heaven who heard their prayers.

- The showbread had special significance. Usually, there were twelve loaves of unleavened bread in two piles of six laid on a special table. They symbolized the fact that every person's daily bread is totally dependent on God who provides. Fresh loaves replaced the ones that were eaten by the priests on the last day of the week.

- There was a large altar on which burnt offerings were sacrificed morning and evening for the sins of the people every day of the year. The blood of these sacrifices was to be sprinkled on the altar on which the burnt offerings were made.

So, Solomon prepared the Temple for these functions. He also prepared a special inner room in the Temple, called "the Holy of Holies" or the "Most Holy Place." While the Ark of the Covenant was built in the days of Moses, in David's time it was stored in a special tent in Jerusalem. Solomon brought it into the Temple to rest in the Holy of Holies. It symbolized the presence of God with His people. When the Temple was finally completed, the burnt offering was prepared on the newly-constructed altar. Then Solomon stood in front of the altar and prayed a magnificent prayer in which he dedicated the Temple as God's house where He would be worshipped. At the conclusion of this prayer, he invited God's Presence to come down. Now let's read how God responded to Solomon's amazing prayer:

> As soon as Solomon finished his prayer, fire came down from heaven and consumed the burnt offering and the sacrifices, and the glory of the Lord filled the Temple. And the priests could not enter the house of the Lord, because the glory of the Lord filled the Lord's house. When all the people of Israel saw the fire come down and the glory of the Lord on the Temple, they bowed down with their faces to the ground on the pavement and worshiped and gave thanks to the Lord, saying, "For He is good, for His steadfast love endures forever."
> 2 Chronicles 7:1-3 (O.T.)

This is not the first time, nor the last time, when fire came from heaven and consumed the burnt offering. It was done on very special occasions, such as the dedication of the Tent of Meeting in the wilderness in Moses' day, the dedication of the great Temple in the days of Solomon, and in the days of Elijah in the dramatic contest between the false prophets of Baal (a pagan god), and God's prophet, Elijah[39] (1 Kings 18:38, O.T.).

The question is: What is the meaning of this fire? It is the approval of God on the burnt sacrifices, necessarily accompanied by the shedding of blood, that are offered for the sins of the people.

Before we leave the era of Solomon, we need to comment on the participation of the common people in this communal event. On behalf of the people, King Solomon offered 22,000 oxen and 120,000 sheep for sacrifices. This went on for seven days during which all of Israel celebrated the dedication of the Temple of God. Remember what the purpose of the Temple was—it was the place where people could worship God after making their sacrifices of atonement for their sins. At the heart of the sacrificial system is the tremendous emphasis on blood. Review again that very important verse in Leviticus 17:11 (O.T.): "For the life of the flesh is in the blood, and I have given it for you on the altar to make atonement for your souls, for it is the blood that makes atonement by the life."

It started with Adam and Eve, clothed with the skins of animals. Then one of their sons, Abel got the point and offered the best of his flock. After the catastrophic flood, Noah sacrificed animals using burnt offerings as atonement for their sins against the Lord. Then the great patriarchs, Abraham, Isaac, and Jacob, built altars and sacrificed burnt offerings for their sins. This trail of blood

---

[39] See the chapter on Elijah for more information.

continued with Job, David, and Solomon. And it will continue until the time of Jesus—for a thousand years longer.

Chapter 14

Jonah

For these next few chapters, we will review and understand the lives and roles of several prophets, beginning with this very unique character, Jonah.

In the Quran

In the first two Quranic references, Jonah (*Yunnus*, also *Jonas*) is mentioned with many others in the prophetic line. For example, in Q. 4:163, we read:

> We have sent thee inspiration, as We sent it to Noah and the Messengers after him: We sent inspiration to Abraham, Isma'il, Isaac, Jacob and to the descendants [the twelve tribes of Israel], to Jesus, Job, Jonah, Aaron, and Solomon, and to David We gave the Psalms.

Similarly, in Q. 6:86, this verse occurs in a list of prophets: "And Isma'il and Elisha, and Jonah and Lot: and to all We gave favor above the nations…"

In Q. 10:98, the Quran refers to a specific incident in the life of Jonah:

Why was there not a single township (among those We warned), which believed—so its faith should have profited it—except the People of Jonah? When they believed, We removed from them the Penalty of Ignominy in the life of the Present, and permitted them to enjoy (their life) for a while.

It is in the last reference to Jonah in the Quran that we read more of a narrative:

So also was Jonah among those sent (by Us). When he ran away (like a slave from captivity) to the ship (fully) laden, he (agreed to) cast lots, and he was condemned: Then the big Fish did swallow him, and he had done acts worthy of blame. Had it not been that he (repented and) glorified Allah, he would certainly have remained inside the Fish till the Day of Resurrection. But We cast him forth on the naked shore in a state of sickness, and We caused to grow, over him, a spreading plant of the Gourd kind. And We sent him (on a mission) to a hundred thousand (men) or more. And they believed; so We permitted them to enjoy (their life) for a while.
Q. 37:139-148

These four passages are all that is written about this reluctant prophet.

In the Bible

Among the prophets of God, Jonah has called worldwide attention to himself because of his unusual experience of being swallowed by a huge fish, living three days and three nights in its belly, and then, at the word of the Lord, was spat out on dry land. His story is recorded in the Old Testament in the book of Jonah (chapters 1-4), and is referred to again by Jesus in the New Testament.

The word of the Lord came to Jonah, and through the word of God, the king of Israel[40] expanded the borders of Israel to its greatest extent (2 Kings 14:25, O.T.). Therefore, it is easy to imagine how popular he was among his own people for helping to bring greatness to his nation. Through Jonah God chose to show His love even to the enemy of His own people. After such an illustrious and long career, God appointed him to preach to non-Jews in the famous city of Nineveh in the country of Assyria. The Assyrians were formerly a great empire and were famous for their excessive cruelty to all of its conquered peoples.

But more recently, in Jonah's time, they were weakened by many civil wars and, consequently, many famines. The year before Jonah was sent to Nineveh there was a total eclipse of the sun[41], and that event terrified the people. In other words, they were now at peace with all their neighbors. This would have allowed the prophet of Israel to preach to his former enemies.

---

[40] Jeroboam II, 782-753 BC.
[41] It occurred on June 16, 763 BC.

But Jonah was a rebellious and prejudiced man, who wished evil on his enemies. He initially refused to show God's compassion to these people and fled from the presence of the Lord. Instead of going to Nineveh he went to the coast and got on board a ship going to Tarshish.

Tarshish was a city somewhere on the coast of the western area of the Mediterranean Sea. What was God going to do with such a hateful, runaway prophet? Because of this rebel prophet, God sent a terrible storm over the sea. To save the ship, the sailors threw their cargo overboard in the midst of the storm, yet the storm grew worse.

That was when every sailor began to pray to his own pagan god. Meanwhile, Jonah was asleep down in the lower deck of the ship. The captain found him and asked why he was not calling on his god.

Then the sailors cast lots (a game of chance) to see who was to blame for this storm. The lot fell on Jonah. The sailors asked him who he was, where he was from, and what he had done wrong. Jonah said he was a Hebrew who worshipped the real God who created heaven and earth and the seas. The sailors became exceedingly afraid and asked Jonah what they should do to quiet the storm. Jonah told them they should throw him into the sea and then the sea would become quiet.

The sailors refused to kill Jonah by throwing him overboard. They rowed even harder, and the storm grew even worse. The sailors did an amazing thing: Instead of calling on their idol gods, for the first time in their lives they called on the real God for forgiveness for throwing this man into the sea. Then they threw Jonah into the sea. The storm immediately quieted down.

Now we get to the main point of this story with regard to our theme of sacrifices of atonement. Even these idolatrous sailors stopped praying to their idols and prayed to the true Creator, Redeemer God who spared their lives. "Then the men feared the Lord exceedingly, and they offered a sacrifice to the Lord and made vows" (Jonah 1:16). As you can see, the trail of sacrifices keeps running all through these stories from the past.

But God is in charge—always—He was not yet finished with Jonah. He prepared a huge fish that swallowed Jonah. While he was in the fish's stomach, deep in the sea, Jonah began to pray to God for mercy. God heard him and commanded the fish to spit him out onto dry land. Then God instructed Jonah a second time to go to Nineveh. This is what he preached: "In forty days Nineveh will be destroyed." Amazingly, the people repented. As a result, God spared the people.

This upset Jonah, who wanted to see the people of Nineveh destroyed. Unlike God, he had no love in his heart for these foreign people. After delivering the message and witnessing their repentance, he then sat in a shady booth (shelter) to watch Nineveh's destruction. It didn't happen. Jonah was so angry he was ready to die. In the middle of his complaining, God asked a profound question of this rebellious prophet: "And should not I pity Nineveh, that great city, in which there are more than 120,000 persons who do not know their right hand from their left, and also much cattle?" (Jonah 4:11, O.T.)

Not only was Nineveh the recipient of God's mercy, He also had mercy on the sailors, and then on Jonah in the stomach of the fish. God loves His creation and "is patient...not wishing that any should perish, but that all should reach repentance" (2 Peter 3:9, N.T.).

God's longing for all to repent so that they would not perish is the reason He continually sent messenger after messenger to declare His will and His desires for the people. In that context, let's move on to two notable prophets by the names of Elijah and Elisha.

Chapter 15

Elijah and Elisha

These two men are responsible for some of the most powerful miracles in history, and many of the most diverse supernatural events ever recorded. Elijah and Elisha, mentor and mentee, were men of renown and power. Their words, works and prophecies caused kings to fear and others to rejoice. Both men are worthy of closer examination.

In the Quran

Here we quote the two passages in the Quran that mention Elijah (*Elias*), Q. 6:84b-85, and Q. 37:122-132:

> We guided Noah and among his progeny...and Jesus and Elias: All in the ranks of the Righteous.
>
> For they (Moses and Aaron) were two of Our believing Servants. So also was Elias among those sent (by Us). Behold, he (Elijah) said to his people (the Israelites), "Will ye not fear (Allah)? Will ye call upon Baal (a pagan god) and forsake the Best of Creators, Allah, your Lord and Cherisher and the Lord and Cherisher of your fathers of old?" But

they rejected him, and they will certainly be called up (for punishment), except the chosen servants of Allah (among them). And we left (this blessing) for him among generations (to come) in later times: "Peace and salutation to such as Elias" (Elijah).

In the Bible

If ever there was an unusual prophet of God, it was Elijah. His life as told in the Bible is located in the Old Testament book of 1 Kings, chapters 17 through 22, concluding in 2 Kings, chapters 1 and 2 (O.T.). Below is a summary of these passages as it relates to the content of this book.

Elijah was from an obscure village in Israel east of the Jordan River. God chose this mighty prophet of faith to challenge the reigning King of Israel for his abandonment of God. The king's name was Ahab. Ahab made the worst possible choice by marrying a woman, Jezebel, who hated God and worshiped Baal, a false Canaanite god. King Ahab set up an altar to Baal in the Temple of God. He also set up a pole symbolizing female fertility, which led to gross immorality.

God inspired Elijah to confront King Ahab. Elijah declared under God's inspiration that there would be no rain for the next few years. Then the Lord led Elijah to hide by a stream east of the Jordan River, where ravens brought meat and bread to feed him until the stream dried up.

Then the Lord directed him to go the town of Zarephath of Sidon where a widow would take care of him. This widow was getting ready to cook her last meal. There was no more food because of the predicted drought and resulting famine. Elijah prayed for her oil and flour to be miraculously replenished day by day, and it was done just as he had prayed.

While living as a guest of that widow, the widow's son died. Elijah took the dead boy up to his chamber and asked the Lord to give back the boy's life. God heard the prayer of this remarkable prophet and gave life back to the boy. By this Elijah proved that he was a genuine man of God who served the true God.

In the third year of the drought and famine, God instructed Elijah to go meet King Ahab, who was searching for Elijah to kill him. Throughout the famine, Jezebel, the queen, was busy killing the prophets of God. Elijah risked his life to confront the king. He accused the king of abandoning the Lord's commands and following the false god, Baal. Elijah challenged the king to bring the people of Israel to the top of Mount Carmel, along with the 450 prophets of Baal, and the 400 prophets of the fertility goddess.

There on Mount Carmel Elijah called for the people to choose either to worship Baal or the true God. Elijah ordered two bulls to be brought for burnt offerings: one to be offered by the prophets of Baal, and the other to be offered by Elijah. The test would be to call fire down from heaven to burn up the offering to Baal, or to call fire down from heaven from the true God.

Elijah let the prophets of Baal go first. All day long these false prophets cried out to Baal, even cutting themselves with knives. No answer came for them. Then at the appointed time of the evening sacrifice, according to the Law of Moses, Elijah built a proper altar, put the wood and the sacrificial animal on it, then commanded the servants to dump water over the sacrifice three times. Then he prayed this mighty prayer:

> O Lord God of Abraham, Isaac and Israel [Jacob's other name], let it be known this day that You are God in Israel and that I am Your servant and have done all these things at Your word. Answer me, O Lord, answer me, so that this people may know that You, O Lord, are God, and that You have turned their hearts back.
> 1 Kings 18:36-37 (O.T.)

Then the fire of the Lord fell and consumed *everything* there—the animal, the wood, the stones of the altar, and the water. The people fell on their faces and said, "The Lord, He is God, the Lord, He is God."

What is the great significance of this overwhelming display of God's approval of the rebuilding of the altar of God and the observance of this evening sacrifice, according to the Law of Moses? It is nothing less than the recovery of God's people from the slavery of idolatry. God was the One who designed this arrangement for the forgiveness of sins. This is an emphatic statement by fire that God was reinstating the true worship and reverence for Himself as the only God and Savior of all mankind. It is a refocusing on the trail of blood that will lead to the final and ultimate sacrifice.

Here is what followed this display of God's awesome power on Mount Carmel: Elijah gave orders to seize the false prophets of Baal and had them all slain. Then Elijah prayed that God would send rain after the three-and-a-half years of drought. God answered the prayers of this powerful prophet of God. The rains came.

After this time, King Ahab sinned again by killing an innocent man and confiscating his beautiful gardens. Later on, Ahab was killed in battle, and Ahab's queen, Jezebel, was thrown out of her palace window and eaten by dogs, as Elijah had prophesied.

Before Elijah was taken to heaven, he was directed by the Lord to appoint Elisha, his disciple and assistant, to succeed him in the prophetic office in Israel.

The most startling thing of all was the fantastic way God took Elijah home to heaven—in a whirlwind accompanied with the appearance of a chariot and horses of fire. Elijah never died. He appears again in the life of Jesus.

Elisha in the Quran

In Q. 6:86, Elisha (*Al Yasa*) is mentioned: "And Ismail and Elisha and Jonas and Lot: to all We gave favour above the nations."

In Q. 38:48, we read, "And commemorate Isma'il, Elisha and *Zul-kifl* [Ezekiel]: Each of them was of the company of the Good."

Elisha in the Bible

Elisha's biography as recalled in the Bible, is found in 1 Kings, chapter 19, and again in 2 Kings, chapters 2 through 13 (O.T.). The most important thing to notice about Elisha is what happened when God called this wealthy man into his service. Let's look at how the Scripture describes it:

> So he [Elijah] departed from there [a cave where God spoke to him] and found Elisha the son of Shaphat, who was plowing with twelve yoke of oxen in front of him, and he was with the twelfth. Elijah passed by him and cast his cloak upon him. And he left the oxen and ran after Elijah and said, "Let me kiss my father and my mother, and then I will follow you." And [Elijah] said to him, "Go back again, for what have I done to you?" And [Elisha] turned from following him and took the yoke of oxen and sacrificed them and boiled their flesh with the yokes of the oxen and gave it to the people, and they ate. Then he arose and went after Elijah and assisted him.
> 1 Kings 19:19-21 (O.T.)

Can you find the trail of blood in this story? At first, you might think it is the communal meal with his family and friends. But that would leave God out of the picture. All of these servants were God-fearing men. For them every event starts and ends with God. So don't miss the meaning of the sacrifice. Elisha ritually slew his yoke of oxen, that is, he shed their blood. He then offered them as a sacrifice. The blood was what made an atonement for his soul. A true servant of God was always conscious of God.

He also was aware that he was a normal human being who, like the rest of us, sinned. Remember, no one is ever able to say, "I have never sinned." God taught that this was His chosen way for humans to be reconciled to God—through the shedding of the blood of a sacrifice for atonement.

If you would like to read further about these two compelling prophets, we recommend that you read 2 Kings 2:1-13:21 (O.T.).

The next prophet we will look at was not a worker of miracles, but was a man moved by God to communicate some of the most dynamic prophecies ever uttered.

Chapter 16

Isaiah

When the Quran uses the term "prophets" to mean those in "the Book" (Bible), it is referring to a set of seventeen men who have books in the Old Testament that bear their names. Isaiah is one of that set. His writings and prophecies are extremely important for us to consider.

In the Quran

There are two references in the Quran that affirm the revelations to (all) the prophets in Q. 2:136 and 3:84. Since they say virtually say the same thing, we will quote the latter verse:

> Say: "We believe in Allah, and in what has been revealed to us and what was revealed to Abraham, Isma'il, Isaac, Jacob, and the Tribes [the twelve sons of Jacob], and in (the Books) given to Moses, Jesus and the prophets from their Lord..."

There were many prophets of God who came before Christ. The Quran does not mention all of them by name. We have chosen one that is not mentioned by name in the Quran, Isaiah. A large book in the Old Testament was named after him and was written by him as a result of the inspiration of the Holy Spirit. The years of his ministry were approximately 740 to 681 BC. His ministry was half-way between the time of Moses and Jesus.

In the Bible

Why this prophet? Why his book? Good questions. Here is a partial answer. First of all, it offers hope for all sinners through the coming of the Messiah. His prophecies had many things to say about Him.

All of Isaiah's predictions of future events came true. He made prophecies about Israel's future, about the Assyrian and Babylonian empires. But as compelling as these confirmations of history are, that is not our focus. We are only going to look at what he prophesied about Jesus the Messiah. For example, 700 years before Jesus was born, Isaiah prophesied that Jesus the Messiah would be born of a virgin, as stated in Isaiah 7:14b (O.T.), "Behold, the virgin shall conceive and bear a Son, and shall call His name Immanuel."

In the Hebrew language the word "Immanuel" means "God with us." This passage was quoted in the New Testament in the gospel by the Apostle Matthew concerning Jesus' birth, as follows:

> Now the birth of Jesus Christ took place this way. When His mother Mary had been betrothed to Joseph, before they came together she was found to be with child from the Holy Spirit. And her husband Joseph, being a just man and unwilling to

put her to shame, resolved to divorce her quietly. But as he considered these things, behold, an angel of the Lord appeared to him in a dream, saying, "Joseph, son of David, do not fear to take Mary as your wife, for that which is conceived in her is from the Holy Spirit. She will bear a Son, and you shall call His name Jesus, for He will save His people from their sins." All this took place to fulfill what the Lord had spoken by the prophet: "Behold the virgin shall conceive and bear a Son, and they shall call His name Immanuel," (which means, God with us). When Joseph woke from sleep, he did as the angel of the Lord commanded him: he took his wife, but knew her not until she had given birth to a Son. And he called His name Jesus.
Matthew 1:18-23 (N.T.)

There is a lot that is in this quote that may be troubling for you as a Muslim. First of all, the Holy Spirit is really the Spirit of the Living God. He is not a created angel. He is eternal—the Spirit of God. He only has to speak and His will is done, as in this case, causing this godly virgin to conceive with a very special child. God took the initiative in this by giving His Son two names, both of which are highly significant:

1. "Jesus." In the original language, Jesus means "Savior" or "Deliverer." As mentioned in the prophecy above, He is going to save His people from their sins.

2. "Immanuel." This name has a very profound meaning. It literally means "God with us." The full meaning of the word and this event is that this Son

123

will have both a human nature, being born of a woman, and a divine nature, coming from the eternal Spirit of God.

Think about it. God chose to visit this earth in human form to show us what He is really like.

When God determined to live among us, He decided not to live as a powerful ruler, but to live a common life among those he called His friends. The question is: will humankind appreciate God living among us?

The prophet Isaiah was a good observer of human nature. He lived in the midst of human corruption and among violent people. This is what he wrote:

> Their works are works of iniquity,
> and deeds of violence are in their hands.
> Their feet run to evil,
> and they are swift to shed innocent blood;
> their thoughts are thoughts of iniquity;
> desolation and destruction are in their highways.
> The way of peace they do not know,
> and there is no justice in the paths;
> they have made their roads crooked;
> no one who treads on them knows peace.
> Isaiah 59:6b-8 (O.T.)

Consider: today, we live with wars, violence, crime, abuse of fellow humans, etc. What would it be like if God were to live among us and be completely vulnerable? This is what Isaiah wrote 700 years before Jesus, the Messiah, came:

His appearance was so marred, beyond human semblance...
He had no form of majesty that we should look at Him, and
no beauty that we should desire Him.
He was despised and rejected by men;
a Man of sorrows and acquainted with grief...
Surely He has borne our griefs and carried our sorrows,
yet we esteemed Him stricken, smitten by God, and afflicted.
But He was pierced for our transgressions;
He was crushed for our iniquities; upon Him was the chastisement that brought us peace,
and with His wounds we are healed.
All we like sheep have gone astray;
we have turned—every one—to his own way;
and the Lord has laid on Him the iniquity of us all...
like a lamb that is led to the slaughter...
He was cut off from the land of the living...
Yet it was the will of the Lord to crush Him...
[H]is soul makes on offering for guilt...
Out of the anguish of His soul He shall see and be satisfied;
by His knowledge shall the Righteous One, My Servant, make many to be accounted righteous
and He shall bear their iniquities...
[H]e poured out His soul to death
and He was numbered with the transgressors;
yet He bore the sin of many,
and makes intercession for the transgressors.
Isaiah 52:14b; 53:2b-12 (in part) (O.T.)

This is what the prophet Isaiah foresaw concerning the One who was to come as Jesus, the Savior of the world, Immanuel, God with us. No, He did not come as a conquering king—that will come in a later age when He returns as the Messiah on the Day of Judgment. In this age, He came as a Lamb of God to take away the sin of the world. This is the time of salvation. It is a time of humankind's probation—a time when our hearts will be tested to reveal whether we can recognize and accept God's provision for our eternal salvation.

Before we move on to the time of Jesus Christ, we need to ask ourselves: is this part of the trail of blood from Adam to the throne? Yes, it is. Even though there is no actual sacrifice or shedding of blood, this prophecy foretells of such a time and such an event.

One more prophet, Malachi, is important to our study. Let's see what God teaches us through his important revelations.

Chapter 17

Malachi

Malachi is another one of the seventeen prophets with a book bearing his name found in the Old Testament in the Bible. His prophecies concern the coming of John the Baptist and Jesus. Malachi's prophetic writings are relevant, especially because his are the last prophecies given before four hundred years of silence occur prior to the arrival of John the Baptist and Jesus.

In the Quran

Again, the verse we quoted in the last chapter also serves us here:

> Say: "We believe in Allah, and in what has been revealed to us and what was revealed to Abraham, Isma'il, Isaac, Jacob, and the Tribes [the twelve sons of Jacob], and in (the Books) given to Moses, Jesus and the prophets from their Lord…"
> Q. 3:84

In the Bible

This last prophet's name was Malachi, which means "My Messenger." After him, no prophet was raised up for the next four hundred years. Why did prophecy die? Why did God remain silent for four centuries? The Bible doesn't say. But we have a fairly good idea. All of the prophets were sent to turn people from idolatry and blasphemy and show them the true path for the way of the righteous, but the people consistently rebelled against God and his prophets. Malachi was the last voice of God to a people who turned away from God and chose the way of destruction.

Through Malachi, God accused the rebellious people of dishonoring God. In what ways were these people defying God? And what has this got to do with the trail of blood? Plenty!

The people's rebellion was four-fold:

- It was an attack on the sacrificial system that achieved atonement between God and men;

- It was an attack on the integrity of the family who were supposed to reflect the image of God;

- It was a corruption of the moral system by calling evil good; and

- It was a violation of the financial system that was designed to support the priesthood and the maintenance of God's central place of worship—the Temple.

Let's take a look at these evil practices that led to the cessation of prophecy.

Through Malachi, God raised this question: "A son honors his father, and a servant his master. If I am a Father, where is My honor? And if I am a Master, where is My fear? says the Lord of Hosts to you, O priests, who despise My name" (Malachi 1:6, O.T.).

The priests pretended to be surprised by these questions and asked in verse 6, "How have we despised Your name?"

God replied through the prophet, "By offering polluted food upon My altar" (Malachi 1:7). They sacrificed blind animals, and others that were lame or sick. This was evil; it did not show proper love or respect for God. Instead, these animals were deformed, sickly, imperfect. God did not accept such despicable sacrifices. He declared His mighty purpose: "From the rising of the sun to its setting, My name will be great among the nations, and in every place incense will be offered to My name...For My name shall be great among the nations..." (Malachi 1:11, O.T.).

God's Temple was meant to be a showcase for the world. His priests were to be holy. The sacrifices were to be perfect. The whole world was to see His greatness and the wisdom of His way of redeeming mankind. The blood of perfect sacrifices was to symbolically wash away the sins of man. As the Scriptures stated, the priests should have guarded this knowledge and properly instructed the worshipers as to the correct meaning of the sacrifices. The priests failed to keep the terms of the Law of Moses. The result was that the people were corrupted, the Temple was profaned, and God was dishonored in the eyes of the world.

Next, the people destroyed their families. They did this in two ways:

- The men of God lusted after idolatrous women and married them. They broke their covenant with God.

- Then they destroyed their families by divorcing their wives, thus ruining their children. Read what the Lord said about this in Malachi 2:14-15 (O.T.):

> [T]he Lord was witness between you and the wife of your youth, to whom you have been faithless, though she is your companion and your wife by covenant. Did He [God] not make them one, with a portion of the [Holy] Spirit in their union? And what was the one God seeking? Godly offspring. So guard yourselves in your spirit, and let none of you be faithless to the wife of your youth.

Not only did these disobedient priests profane the Temple, but they contributed to the destruction of family life by neglecting to teach what the word of God said about the sanctity of marriage and the raising of children in the knowledge and reverence of God. At least five hundred years before Malachi, King Solomon wrote the following words in the book of Proverbs:

The fear of the Lord is the beginning of knowledge, fools despise wisdom and instruction.

The fear of the Lord is the beginning of wisdom, and the knowledge of the Holy One is insight. For by Me your days will be multiplied, and years will be added to your life.
Proverbs 1:7 and 9:10-11 (O.T.)

Now let's read about the third failure of these supposedly believing people who called evil good.

God charged them with wearing Him out with their evil. Being self-deceived by their own sin, they told the Lord that they were not making Him weary. They thought they were quite religious by going through the required rituals.

God was not deceived by their hypocrisy. Read what He said to these hypocritical citizens in His kingdom:

"Then I will draw near to you in judgment. I will be a swift witness against the sorcerers, against the adulterers, against those who swear falsely, against those who oppress the hired worker in his wages, the widow and the fatherless, against those who thrust aside the sojourner, and do not fear Me," says the Lord of Hosts.
Malachi 3:5 (O.T.)

Let's summarize so far what all the people did in dishonoring God. They brought diseased animals to the corrupt priests, who accepted them and offered them for sacrifice. These priests are the ones who turned godly families into godless ones by failing to teach them the word of the Lord. They approved of the believers marrying non-believers, and they approved of divorce.

To the above list of their various sins, there is one more to be added: their love of money, their greed. This impoverished the maintenance of the Temple, it contributed to the corruption of the sacrificial system, and it failed to contribute to the salaries of the priest. On this point, God charged them with robbing Him: they refused to give the tithe (one tenth of their income) to God. Their greed undermined every aspect of worship, thus ruining God's name in the sight of the nations. No wonder the voice of prophecy went silent for four hundred years. The people of God from the time of Moses (1400 BC) to the time of Malachi (about 400 BC), had been rebelling against the word of God.

As a result of a thousand years of dereliction of their duty (with some exceptions), it looked like God withdrew, on the surface, from all prophetic activity. In reality, He was preparing His people for the great display of His love, His wisdom, and His righteousness in the redemption of mankind. He was going to raise up a prophet to prepare the world for His greatest surprise:

> "Behold, I send My messenger [John the Baptist], and he will prepare the way before Me. And the Lord whom you seek will suddenly come to His Temple; and the Messenger of the covenant [Jesus] in whom you delight, behold, He is coming," says the Lord of hosts.
> Malachi 3:1 (O.T.)

"Behold, I will send Elijah the prophet before that great and awesome day of the Lord comes."
Malachi 4:5 (O.T.)

These two prophecies of Malachi are actually about John the Baptist and Jesus. In the New Testament, we learn that Elijah came in the form of John the Baptist, the son of Zechariah, the forerunner of Jesus. And so we turn to the next chapter to see how his story fits into the trail of blood.

Chapter 18

Zechariah and His Son, John the Baptist

After 400 years of silence, God sent His angel, Gabriel, to a priest by the name of Zechariah, telling him that in his old age, he and his barren wife were going to have a son, the prophet John (the Baptist), who would be the forerunner of the Messiah.

Zechariah in the Quran

Here is a summary of the Quranic references to Zechariah (*Zakariya*):

- It is said that Zechariah was in charge of taking care of Mary, the mother of Jesus (Q. 3:37). One day he was in his chamber praying, asking Allah for an heir, even though he and his wife were old and past the age of having children. Allah answered his prayer by sending an angel to give him glad tidings of a baby boy who would be called John (*Yahya*). Zechariah had trouble believing this and asked God for a sign. The sign that was given was that Zechariah would not be able to speak for three days and three nights (Q. 3:38-41; 19:2-11).

- The Lord cured his wife of barrenness. Zechariah exhorted the people to praise Allah and give him glory (Q. 21:89-90).

- He was listed as among the prophets of Allah (Q. 6:85).

Zechariah in the Bible

In the Biblical account (Luke 1:5-24, 57-80, N.T.), we find many more details of the story of Zechariah. He is described as very devout and a God-fearing priest. He was chosen by lot (that is, by chance) to go into the Holy of Holies of the great Temple and burn incense before the Lord.[42]

While he was performing his duty as a priest in the Holy of Holies, the angel Gabriel appeared to him and informed him that the Lord had heard his prayer and that his wife, Elizabeth, although very old, was going to have a son, whose name was to be John. Zechariah asked Gabriel how this could be, since he and his wife were old and past the time of having children. As a result of his doubting, Gabriel said that Zechariah would not be able to speak again until the child was born. When he came out of the Temple, he was unable to speak.

Approximately one year later, his wife bore a child. The relatives wanted to name the baby Zechariah, after the father, but Elizabeth said no, his name was to be John. Then they asked Zechariah what to name him; he called

---

[42] The burning of incense morning and evening represented the prayers of the believers ascending to God.

for a writing tablet and wrote that his name was to be John. Immediately, Zechariah was able to speak again. He was filled with the Holy Spirit and began to prophesy. His prophecy was in the form of a Hebrew poem:

> "Blessed be the Lord God of Israel, for He has visited and redeemed His people and has raised up a horn of salvation for us in the house of His servant David, as He spoke by the mouth of His holy prophets from of old..."
> Luke 1:68-70 (N.T.)

Even though there is no direct mention of blood in this prophecy, it is implied in the use of the words "redeemed" and "salvation." Let us explain: the words "redeem," "redeemed," "redeemer" and "redemption" have a long history in the Bible. The words occur 157 times, as recorded in twenty-nine of the sixty-six books that make up the entire Bible, both in the Old and the New Testaments. In fact, one or the other of these words occurs in the first book of the Bible (Genesis) and the last book (Revelation). It is true that these words have a wide variety of meanings. But the basic meaning is to set free by paying some kind of a price, usually a sacrifice. In other words, a life can be redeemed by offering an appropriate sacrifice. Of course, these redemptive sacrifices involved the shedding of the blood of a sacrificial animal on behalf of the one to be redeemed. As a priest, Zechariah knew very well that the job of the priests was to slay the animals and sacrifice them on the altar as a burnt offering.

Zechariah, in his great prophetic poem, also mentioned the word "salvation." Here are the exact words in the English translation: "And you, child [John], will be called the prophet of the Most High; / for you will go before the Lord to prepare His ways, / to give knowledge of salvation to His people / in the forgiveness of their sins" (Luke 1:76-77, N.T.).

In these momentous words, we find "salvation" means the forgiveness of sins. When we go back to the Law of Moses, we remember the costly sacrifices of animals that were offered up as sin offerings on behalf of the sins of the person making the sacrifice. This is what every human being is looking for—the forgiveness of his or her sins. In fact, the whole world is looking for this redemption, this salvation, this promise of the forgiveness of one's offenses. The question is: what will be the basis of this mercy of God in granting forgiveness to sinners? How will the Most High, also called "the Lord" in this prophecy, accomplish this salvation for the people?

In Zechariah's day, this long-expected Redeemer was also called the Messiah.[43] Remember Job's great statement of faith when he was being tested:

> For I know that my Redeemer lives,
> and at the last He will stand upon the earth.
> And after my skin has been thus destroyed,
> yet in my flesh I shall see God,
> whom I shall see for myself,
> and my own eyes shall behold, and not another.
> My heart faints within me!
> Job 19:25-27 (O.T.)

---

[43] Messiah means "the Anointed One."

This Messiah was understood to be the Redeemer, the Savior who would save His people from their sins.

Zechariah understood that his son, John, was going to prepare the way for the coming of the Messiah, called Redeemer and Savior. What catches our attention here in this prophecy is that the Messiah is also called "Lord."

John the Baptist in the Quran

There are only seven verses in the Quran concerning John. His coming birth was announced to his father Zechariah (Q. 19:7; 3:39; 21:90) and he would be a witness to the word of truth from God. His name is included in a list of the prophets mentioned in the Quran (Q. 6:85). He was described as devout, as kind to his parents and was exhorted to take firm hold of the Book and he would be given wisdom. Then this benediction was pronounced on John: "Peace would be on him the day he was born, on the day he would die, and on the day he would be raised up again" (Q. 19:12-15).

John the Baptist in the Bible

When we turn to the material in the Bible on John the Baptist, many interesting details are mentioned in several of the books that make up the New Testament, the collection of books that is called the *"Injil"* in the Quran. Listed below are highlights of these references to John the Baptist:

In those days John the Baptist came preaching in the wilderness of Judea, "Repent, for the kingdom of heaven is at hand." For this is he who was spoken of by the prophet Isaiah[44] when he said,
> "The voice of one crying in the wilderness:
> 'Prepare the way of the Lord;
> make His paths straight.'"

Matthew 3:1-3 (N.T.)

Then we have these words of John himself: "I baptize you with water for repentance [of sins], but He who is coming after me is mightier than I, whose sandals I am not worthy to carry. He will baptize you with the Holy Spirit and fire[45]" (Matthew 3:11, N.T.).

There are just two other points that we should remember from this prophecy by John, and they are, first, that the kingdom of heaven (also called the kingdom of God) is about to be introduced by Jesus; and second, that the person that John is preparing the way for is called the Lord.

In the Gospel of Luke, the prophecy of Isaiah is again mentioned, but with a few more details:

> "The voice of one crying in the wilderness:
> 'Prepare the way of the Lord, make His paths straight.
> Every valley shall be filled,
> and every mountain and hill shall be made low,

---

[44] 740-700 BC

[45] Historically, the Holy Spirit would be given to believers on the day of Pentecost and from that day onward. The reference to "fire" refers to purification.

and the crooked shall become straight,
and the rough places shall become level ways,
and all flesh shall see the salvation of God.'"
Luke 3:4b-6 (N.T.)

What interests us in this passage are the words, "All flesh shall see the salvation of God." What is this salvation? What are the people going to be saved from? As this book progresses, the answers to such questions will become apparent.

As we continue with this material on John the Baptist, we now turn to the book in the New Testament that is called the "Gospel of John." This John is one of Jesus' apostles and is not to be confused with John the Baptist. In this gospel, this is what we read of John the Baptist and the one about whom he came to bear witness:

> There was a man sent from God, whose name was John. He came as a witness, to bear witness about the Light, that all might believe through Him. He was not the Light, but came to bear witness about the Light. The true Light, which gives light to everyone, was coming into the world. He was in the world, and the world was made through Him, yet the world did not know Him. He came to His own, and His own people did not receive Him. But to all who did receive Him, who believed in His name, He gave the right to become children of God, who were born, not of blood nor of the will of the flesh, nor of the will of man, but of God.
> John (the apostle, not the Baptist) 1:6-13 (N.T.)

There are more new and startling concepts in this passage. What is implied is that John the Baptist was preparing the way for the One who was going to be called "the Light of the World." Then we read the amazing words that those who believe in the Light will be born [again] of God and, hence, be called the children of God. For you, the reader, these, no doubt, are entirely new ideas. So, we ask you to be patient as we unfold the Scriptures that the Quran confirms.

Before leaving the material related to John the Baptist there is one more incident that we must introduce because it holds the key to God's entire plan for the future of humankind. This is what we are referring to:

> The next day [John the Baptist] saw Jesus coming toward him, and said, "Behold, the Lamb of God, who takes away the sin of the world! This is He of whom I said, 'After me comes a man who ranks before me'...I myself did not know Him but for this purpose I came baptizing with water that He might be revealed to Israel."
>
> "I myself did not know Him, but He who sent me to baptize with water said to me, 'He on Whom you see the Spirit descend and remain, this is He who baptizes with the Holy Spirit.' And I have seen and borne witness that this is the Son of God."
> John 1:29-31, 33-35 (N.T.)

Dear friend, we know how puzzling this baptism of the Holy Spirit must be to you and how shocking it must be to read that a prophet, *Yahya*, John the Baptist, who is listed in the Quran, would call Jesus "the Son of God." Before you turn away, please remember how many times the Quran says it came to confirm the previous Scriptures.[46] These are the Scriptures that were in existence, uncorrupted, and unchanged in the days when the Quran was given. We know this is not what you have been taught. But we beg you to review the material at the beginning of this book that shows that these Scriptures have not been changed or corrupted.

If you will be patient, we hope to show you as you finish reading this book (and we trust that you will read it through completely), how logical the teachings of the Bible are. You will be mightily blessed if you stick with us and read to the end. After all, this whole work is about how we all can receive the forgiveness of our sins and not be sent to a frightening hell on Judgment Day.

"Blessed is the one who reads aloud the words of this prophecy, and blessed are those who hear, and who keep what is written in it, for the time is near" (Revelation 1:3, N.T.).

---

[46] See chapter "The Bible Affirmed by the Quran and Other Sources."

Chapter 19

Jesus: In Old Testament Prophecies

Our journey along this trail of blood brings us to a Person born as the result of a miracle; a Person of perfect character; a Person of incredible power; and a Person who suffered immensely while He was here upon this planet. And He is a Person who is coming to Earth again. This Person is Jesus.

In the Quran

Jesus (*Isa*) is by far the most engaging personality in the Quran. Look at Jesus' description in some of the ninety-three verses spread over fourteen suras. Jesus is called and presented as follows:

- He is the Word of Allah (Q. 4:171).

- He is a Spirit from Allah (Q. 4:171).

- He is righteous (sinless) (Q. 3:46).

- The Jews claimed that they killed Christ Jesus (*Isa al-Masih*) (on the cross) (Q. 4:157).

- Allah raised Jesus to himself (Q. 4:158).

- Jesus raised the dead, gave sight to those born blind, cured people of leprosy, and created live birds (Q. 5:110).

- He was a mercy from Allah (Q. 19:21).

- He was born of the virgin Mary by the mighty power of Allah (Q. 19:20, 22).

- He prophesied His own death and resurrection (Q. 19:33).

- He was called a sign for all peoples (Q. 21:91).

- Jesus' coming will be a sign of the Day of Judgment (Q. 43:61).

These verses portray an exceptional description of Jesus, who was like no other.

Prophecy in the Bible

In this section, we will look at the prophecies found in the Old Testament. Some of this will be review and some will be new material.

Prophetic Action in the Days of Abraham

Abraham lived in troubled times that took place 2,000 years before Christ. To the east of him there was a war that impacted the future of his nephew, Lot (*Lut*). A coalition of four powerful armies from the north invaded the land of Canaan, conquered it, and carried off the plunder and some of the people, including Abraham's nephew, Lot, and Lot's family. Abraham mobilized his trained fighters and pursued the northern armies. In a surprise attack, he succeeded in defeating the armies, and recovered his nephew. Abraham also recovered all their property. When he returned from the battle, he was met by the king of Salem (which means "peace") who was named Melchizedek (whose name means "King of Righteousness"). He was the priest of the Most High God. Melchizedek brought bread and wine to victorious Abraham (Genesis 14:1-24, O.T.).

This story may seem irrelevant, except that King David, who a thousand years later prophesied about the coming of the Lord, linked Melchizedek to Christ in Psalm 110:1, 4 (O.T.): "The Lord says to my Lord: / 'Sit at my right hand, until I make your enemies your footstool... / You are a priest forever after the order of Melchizedek.'"[47]

In this prophecy, as explained in the New Testament, "the Lord" (not "*my* Lord") in this passage refers to Jesus. The inspired writer of the book of Hebrews in the New Testament also applied the name of Melchizedek to Jesus (Hebrews 5:6, N.T.). He said, speaking of Jesus: "You are a priest forever after the order of Melchizedek."

Thus, Jesus is proclaimed as an eternal priest of the Most High God. What is the function of a priest? The answer is two-fold: The priest is an intermediary between God and

---

[47] Melchizedek had no beginning and no end (see Hebrews 7:3, N.T.).

humans. On God's behalf, he proclaims the word of God to people, and on behalf of people he offers sacrifice to God. Jesus fulfilled both roles. This establishes Jesus as an eternal Priest, in addition to His other roles.

Moses' Prophecy

> The Lord said to me [Moses, fourteen hundred years before Christ]…"I [God] will raise up for them [the Israelites] a prophet like you from among their brothers. And I will put My words in His mouth and He shall speak to them all that I command Him."
> Deuteronomy 18:17-18 (O.T.)

Some of our Muslim friends try to claim this is a prophecy about their prophet, but it is not. Moses was speaking to his brothers, the twelve tribes of Israel. Jesus, on His human side, descended from Judah, one of the twelve tribes. There are two passages that demonstrate the fulfillment of this prophecy by Jesus. Let's look at these two quotes in the New Testament.

This is how the Apostle Peter used this passage in his first sermon, applying the prophecy to Jesus after the Holy Spirit came upon Peter:

> "Moses said, 'The Lord God will raise up for you a prophet like me [Moses] from your brothers. You shall listen to Him in whatever He tells you. And it shall be that every soul who does not listen to that prophet [Jesus] shall be destroyed from the people.'"

Acts 3:22-23 (N.T.)

This is how Stephen, the first Christian martyr, used this prophecy in his defense in his testimony about Jesus:

> "This is the Moses who said to the Israelites, 'God will raise up a prophet [understood to be Jesus in fulfillment of the original prophecy] like me [Moses] from your brothers.'"[48]
> Acts 7:37 (N.T.)

David's Prophecies

The first and most startling prophecy is in the second Psalm (*Zabur*). It was originally applied to King David when he was installed as king: "'As for me, I [God] have set My King on Zion, My holy hill.' I [David] will tell of the decree: The Lord said to me, 'You are my Son; today I have begotten You'" (Psalm 2:6-7, O.T.).

This is quoted a thousand years later in the book of Hebrews 1:5-6, 8 (N.T.), and applied to Jesus:

> [T]o which of the angels did God ever say, "You are My Son, today I have begotten You" [first stated in Psalm 2:7, O.T.]?

> But of the Son He says, "Your throne, O God, is forever and ever..." [first stated in Psalm 45:6, O.T.]

---

[48] We have inserted the information in the bracket because the Apostle Peter and the spirit-filled servant Stephen recognized that Jesus was the true fulfillment of this prophecy.

It is a lot to think about. Jesus in prophecy is called "God's Son." In the Psalms, the Son is also called "God" and on His throne He will reign forever. Who is this Jesus? We think you will discover He is more than a prophet. Next, let's revisit the prophet Isaiah.

Isaiah's Prophecies (700 years BC)

We have already referred to this amazing prophecy in the "Isaiah" chapter of this book:

> "Hear then, O house of David! Is it too little for you to weary men, that you weary my God also? Therefore the Lord Himself will give you a sign. Behold, the virgin shall conceive and bear a Son, and shall call His name Immanuel."
> Isaiah 7:13-14 (O.T.)

Our God is a communicating God, and by His angel, Gabriel, He spoke to Joseph, the husband-to-be of the virgin Mary, in a dream, and He revealed two astounding things to Joseph about the coming Son:

> "She will bear a Son, and you shall call His name Jesus, for He will save His people from their sins." All this took place to fulfill what the Lord had spoken by the prophet [Isaiah]: "Behold, the virgin shall conceive and bear a Son, and they shall call His name Immanuel," which means, "God with us" [from Isaiah 7:14, O.T.].
> Matthew 1:21-23 (N.T.)

This next prophecy of Isaiah, inspired by the Holy Spirit, made an even more startling declaration:

> For to us a child is born,
> to us a Son is given;
> and the government shall be upon His shoulder,
> and His name shall be called
> Wonderful Counselor, Mighty God,
> Everlasting Father, Prince of Peace.
> Of the increase of His government and of peace
> there will be no end,
> on the throne of David and over His kingdom,
> to establish it and uphold it
> with justice and with righteousness
> from this time forth and forevermore.
> The zeal of the Lord of hosts will do this.
> Isaiah 9:6-7 (O.T.)

Without understanding the being—the essence—of God it would be impossible to make sense of this prophecy, which calls Jesus not only the Son, but also Father, Counselor[49], and God! Over and over again the Bible affirms that God is One. Moses affirmed it. So did David. So did all the prophets. So did Jesus. So did all of Jesus' apostles. So do all Christians today. So what is the key to understanding this prophecy and how it applies to Jesus? The answer is found in God's own revelation of Himself. He is sovereign. He can choose to reveal Himself however He wants to. He is not bound by the finite reasoning of man. He is greater.

---

[49] See John 14:26, (N.T., New International Version), "But the Counselor, the Holy Spirit, whom the Father will send in My name, will teach you all things and will remind you of everything I have said to you."

Let's use an illustration from the Bible itself. On the first page of the Bible, God gave us the clue:

> Then God said, "Let Us make man [Adam] in Our image, after Our likeness..." So God created man in His own image, in the image of God He created him; male and female He created them.
> Genesis 1:26-27 (O.T.)

The best way to understand this is to use the following illustration. By the power of the Holy Spirit, God has chosen to also reveal Himself as love. We have this expression, "God is love."[50] To best illustrate love, in human terms, we use three objects: the lover, the beloved, and the love expressed between them. In this illustration the lover is the Father, the beloved is the Son and the love flowing between them all is the Spirit, all inside the Oneness of God. In the next passages we will see how this love of God expresses Himself to man.

In the Old Testament book of Isaiah 52:13-53:12, we have a deeply moving prophecy of God who chose an unexpected way to express His love to humans. This is one of the four "servant songs" found in Isaiah. Jesus is referred to as a servant in the Quran (4:172; 19:30). But also in the New Testament He is referred to as a servant. Jesus said of Himself that He had come as a servant. We will quote one example that will give us more understanding as we read Isaiah's prophecy. It is located in Mark 10:45 (N.T.): "For even the Son of Man [a Messianic expression] came not to be served but to serve, and to give His life as a ransom for many." And in another passage He

---

[50] Found in 1 John 4:8 and repeated in 1 John 4:16 (N.T.).

described this as a supreme act of love: "Greater love has no one than this, that someone lay down his life for his friends" (John 15:13, N.T.).

Starting about one hundred years before the birth of Jesus, the Jews developed the concept of a coming Savior who was called the Messiah (the "Anointed One," *Masih* in Arabic, *Christos* in Greek, *Christ* in English). The Jews were expecting the Messiah to be a conquering king who would drive the Romans out of Israel and establish the Kingdom of God. They had no idea that the Messiah would be a "Suffering Savior." Nor did they understand the Good News (*Injil*) was going to be about the forgiveness of sin for all who believed in Jesus and who would receive the gift of eternal life.

In this light, let us look at the following "suffering servant song" in Isaiah. For it is about Jesus, who came seven hundred years after this prophecy was made. We will give some selections from the verses of this song:

> He was despised and rejected by men,
> a man of sorrows,
> and acquainted with grief...
> Surely He has borne our griefs and carried our sorrows...
> smitten by God...
> But He was pierced for our transgressions,
> He was crushed for our iniquities...
> and with His wounds we are healed...
> the Lord has laid on Him the iniquity of us all...
> like a lamb that is led to the slaughter...
> Yet it was the will of the Lord to crush Him;
> He has put Him to grief...

His soul makes an offering for guilt...
He shall bear their iniquities...
yet He bore the sin of many,
and makes intercession for the transgressors.
Isaiah 53:3-12 (in part) (O.T.)

Embedded in this song are words that speak of bloodshed. Look again and note these words: smitten, pierced, crushed, wounds, slaughter, offering. Let's see how this is fulfilled in the life of Jesus Christ.

Chapter 20

Jesus: In the Gospels

For this chapter, we will be working in the Holy Spirit-inspired accounts written by the Apostle Matthew, one of the twelve disciples of Jesus; Mark, who worked closely with the Apostle Peter, who was another one of the twelve disciples of Jesus; Luke, a medical doctor and historian who worked closely with the Apostle Paul; and the Apostle John, who was the closest of the twelve disciples to Jesus.[51]

Because the Holy Spirit of God, God's very Spirit, was the one who inspired these writings, the accounts are called inspired Scripture. They have been accepted for the last two thousand years as reliable and genuine reports of events in the life of Jesus. These writings are from four different persons. They reflect the testimony of each author. As one would assume, there is much material that is common to all four. But there is also content in each that is unique to that author. All together, these four books—Matthew, Mark, Luke and John—tell us all we need to know about the life of Jesus, His message, and all that is needed for believing in Him and receiving salvation,

---

[51] Not to be confused with John the Baptist, son of Zechariah,

that is, for the forgiveness of sins and assurance of eternal life.

Since we have already summarized the Quranic material on Jesus in the previous chapter, we will not need to repeat it here. As our theme is the subject of sacrifice, we will restrict our selection of material to that which fits this theme.[52] Let's have a look at what the gospel writers said about Jesus, as well as several direct quotes by Jesus.

The best place to begin is with the words the angel Gabriel spoke to Mary about the coming of her Son:

> "Do not be afraid, Mary, for you have favor with God. And behold, you will conceive in your womb and bear a Son, and you shall call His name Jesus. He will be great and will be called the Son of the Most High. And the Lord God will give to Him the throne of His father David[53], and He will reign over the house of Jacob forever, and of His kingdom there shall be no end."
> Luke 1:30-33 (N.T.)

The angel, Gabriel, answered Mary's question as to how this would happen with this reply, "The Holy Spirit will come upon you, and the power of the Most High will overshadow you; therefore the child to be born will be called holy—the Son of God" (Luke 1:35, N.T.). And later, Gabriel commented, "Nothing will be impossible with God" (Luke 1:37, N.T.).

---

[52] For those who are intrigued with all the other details of Jesus' life, we recommend you follow your interest. It will be very worthwhile.
[53] On the human side Jesus was descended from the line of King David.

This startling visit by Gabriel calls for some explanation. First of all, the angel Gabriel is never to be confused with the Holy Spirit, as some believe. The Holy Spirit is God's eternal spirit, not a created being, as are all angels.

Furthermore, in giving His name as Jesus, which means "Savior" or "Deliverer," it is implied that Jesus will save His people from their sins. How He will do this requires that blood will be shed.

When the infant Jesus was presented in the Temple on the eighth day, according to the Law of Moses, a devout follower named Simeon, led by the Spirit of God, took Jesus in his arms, blessed God, and said to Mary, the mother of Jesus, "Behold, this Child is appointed for the fall and rising of many in Israel, and for a sign that is opposed (and a sword will pierce through your own soul also[54]) ..." (Luke 2:34-35, N.T.).

Subsequently, for the first thirty years of His life, Jesus lived in obscurity. The only exception was when He was twelve years old: He discussed many themes in the Scriptures with scholars in the Temple (Luke 2:41-51, N.T.).

When He was about thirty years of age, before He began His ministry, He came to His cousin, John the Baptist, to be baptized. This is what occurred at His baptism:

> When Jesus was baptized, immediately He went up from the water, and behold, the heavens were

---

[54] From subsequent events, we know that this phrase, "a sword will pierce through you own soul," refers to the coming time when Mary will witness her Son being put to death on the cross.

opened to Him, and He saw the Spirit of God descending like a dove and coming to rest on Him, and behold, a voice from heaven said, "This is My beloved Son, with whom I am well pleased."
Matthew 3:16-17 (N.T.)

Notice the unity, the oneness of the purpose of God in this event: the approving voice of the Father and the anointing presence of His Spirit are involved in the inauguration of the ministry of the Son. For God, who is described as Spirit, to give His divine approval of His Son is an awesome event. The great war between God and Satan over the souls of men was about to begin. It would cost the Son His life, but He would prove to be victorious.

In the gospels, Mark 1:12-13a (N.T.), and Matthew 4:1-11 (N.T.), we read what happened right after the baptism of Jesus: "The Spirit immediately drove Him [Jesus] out into the wilderness. And He was in the wilderness for forty days, being tempted by Satan" (Mark's gospel). And in Matthew: "and fasting forty days and forty nights, He was hungry and the tempter came…" (v. 2). During this time, Satan presented three great temptations. In answer to each one, Jesus replied, "It is written," and He then quoted from memory the appropriate response from Scripture to each temptation. "Then the devil left Him, and behold, angels came and were ministering to Him" (v. 11).[55]

After successfully resisting Satan in this first encounter, Jesus began His ministry of healing, delivering people from demonic oppression, and even raising those who died to life again. During the next three years of ministry

---

[55] We should add that at this point Satan was behind the scenes scheming for the crucifixion of Jesus.

Jesus relentlessly moved to the great climax of His mission. Let's read Jesus' own words: "For even the Son of Man came not to be served but to serve, and to give His life as a ransom for many" (Mark 10:45, N.T.).

Please note: the expression "the Son of Man" was the way Jesus referred to Himself as the representative Man, and "the Son of God" as the way He referred to His deity, His coming down from heaven on His divine mission as the Savior of the world. He is one and the same person with both natures: the human and the divine.

As we have mentioned in a previous chapter, the Scripture states, "God is love" (1 John 4:8, N.T.). Jesus' ministry can be defined as a life of love, of giving Himself in loving service to others, showing compassion to all. One day, Jesus described love in this way: "Greater love has no one than this, that someone lay down his life for his friends" (John 15:13, N.T.).

He gave other clues as to what was going to happen to Him. He used the illustration of Himself as the good shepherd in these words: "I am the good shepherd. The good shepherd lays down his life for his sheep..." and again, "I lay down My life for the sheep" (John 10:11, 15, N.T.).

Jesus tried to prepare His disciples for that fateful day when He would be put on the cross, but the disciples did not understand:

> He was teaching His disciples, saying to them, "The Son of Man is going to be delivered into the hands of men, and they will kill Him. And when He

is killed, after three days He will rise." But they did not understand the saying... (Mark 9:31-32a, N.T.).

For us to understand this divine drama, we are going to need to review material in the Law of Moses, with which you may not be so familiar. Remember the story of Moses in his confrontation with Pharaoh? In the Quran, nine plagues on the Egyptians were mentioned; but in the Bible there is a tenth plague that is mentioned, a plague so terrible that it caused the Egyptians to let the Israelites go free.

God instructed every family of the Israelites to kill a lamb for each household and put its blood on the doorposts and lintels over their doors. God was going to send the Angel of Destruction over all of Egypt and he would kill the firstborn in every house that did not have this blood on its doorframes but would pass over the houses with blood on their doorposts. This led to the annual "Passover" celebration that the Israelites observed every year until the days of Jesus and beyond. By the blood of the sacrificial lamb, every Israelite family was spared this terrible night of death. This occurred 1,400 years before Jesus' time.

As the centuries passed, the Passover celebration evolved to the way it was observed in Jesus' day. A lamb would be killed for every family. The lamb would be roasted. and a specific meal would be prepared, including special bread without yeast. This bread would be broken into pieces and some given to everyone present. At the conclusion, wine would be served, called the "cup of blessing."

Jesus, of course, observed this celebration every year of His life. But the night before He was going to be put on the cross, He did something very unusual. Let's read from the Bible what happened:

> Now on the first day of Unleavened Bread the disciples came to Jesus, saying, "Where will You have us prepare for You to eat the Passover?" He said, "Go into the city to a certain man and say to him, 'The Teacher says, My time is at hand. I will keep the Passover at your house with My disciples.'"...When it was evening, He reclined at table with the twelve [disciples]. And as they were eating, He said, "Truly, I say to you, one of you will betray Me...The Son of Man goes as it is written of Him, but woe to the man by whom the Son of Man is betrayed!"
> Matthew 26:17-18, 20-21, 24a (N.T.)

The betrayal was done by a man named Judas from Judea. Judas was one of Jesus' twelve disciples. Judas was a thief: he was in charge of the bag of money from which the poor were helped, and he stole from it. Satan put it into his heart to betray Jesus. Later that night Satan entered Judas, and he led the soldiers to capture Jesus.

Now back to the scene at the table:

> Now as they were eating, Jesus took bread, and after blessing it broke it and gave to the disciples, and said, "Take, eat, this is My body." And He took a cup, and when He had given thanks He gave it to them, saying, "Drink of it, all of you, for this is My blood of the covenant, which is poured out for

many for the forgiveness of sins. I tell you I will not drink again of this fruit of the vine until that day when I drink it new with you in My Father's kingdom."
Matthew 26:26-29 (N.T.)

This is absolutely shocking. Jesus took a cup of wine and said, "This is my blood. Drink it." This is unthinkable. What does it mean? And He did the same with the unleavened bread. "This is my body. Eat it." It must be symbolic; but what does it symbolize? We must read on and find out. We must make sense of this strange conversation.

Chapter 21

Jesus: The Meaning of His Flesh and Blood
(revised 2021)

Eat Jesus' body? Drink Jesus' blood? How is that possible? First of all, they are metaphors for something we must do, according to what He requires.

Jesus is certainly not asking any of us to literally eat Him or drink His actual blood. That would be absurd and impossible. Even His disciples understood that it was not to be taken literally.

Naturally speaking, what is eating? It is the taking into our bodies that which we have determined to eat. We chew it, we swallow it, then our body digests it and applies the nutrients in all the ways which are needed. The same is true for what we drink. We take it in, we swallow it, and then our bodies' natural processes take over for the sake of digestion and application.

Eating and drinking are essential to living. Without either, we will die.

So, is it so very strange that Jesus would refer to Himself as being essential to having life...eternal life?

Not at all. Listen to His statements about Himself in the

book of John, chapter 6:

> "I am the living bread that came down from Heaven. If anyone eats of this bread, he will live forever. And the bread that I will give for the life of the world is My flesh…Truly, truly, I say to you, unless you eat the flesh of the Son of Man and drink His blood, you have no life in you. Whoever feeds on My flesh and drinks My blood has eternal life, and I will raise him up on the last day. For My flesh is true food, and My blood is true drink. Whoever feeds on My flesh and drinks My blood abides in Me, and I in him. As the living Father sent Me, and I live because of the Father, so whoever feeds on Me, he also will live because of Me…Whoever feeds on this bread will live forever" (John 6:51, 53-57, 58b, N.T.).

These statements from Jesus are a direct revelation of Him being the fulfillment of the type, the imagery, the events of what happened in Exodus chapter 12. In the Exodus passage, the tenth plague was going to take place. This plague was to be the death of all the firstborn throughout the entire land of Egypt. But the Lord made provision for the nation of Israel by instructing them to place the blood of a one-year-old, male lamb—one without defect or blemish--in three places on the doorway of their homes. In addition, they were to prepare and eat that same lamb while they were fully clothed and ready to move. The Lord Himself calls this meal, and that night's event, "the Lord's Passover." Furthermore, this is what God told Moses regarding what was to happen:

"On that same night I [God] will pass through Egypt and strike down every firstborn—both men and animals—and I will bring judgment on all the gods of Egypt. I am the LORD. The blood will be a sign for you on the houses where you are; and when I see the blood, **I will pass over you.** No destructive plague will touch you when I strike Egypt."

Exodus 12:13 (O.T.)

Because of the blood of the lamb, death passed over that household and the lives of those inside were saved. Furthermore, the blood, because of how it was to be placed on the doorframe, foreshadowed the image of a cross. Christ then directly connects Himself in John chapter 6 as the fulfillment of the Passover event when blood saved the lives of all who were protected by it. This is also why the Apostle Paul states, "For Christ, our Passover lamb, has been sacrificed" (1 Corinthians 5:7b, N.T.).

Furthermore, Jesus also refers to Himself as "the living bread that came down from Heaven." This is a direct correlation to God's providing manna for the Israelites so they might not starve while in the wilderness (Exodus chapter 16). This was a miraculous, life-giving provision of God. Jesus clearly tells us that His flesh is the bread that gives eternal life, while the bread (manna) in the wilderness was sufficient for the Israelites' temporal life.

As the Passover lamb, without defect, He gave His life in order that each of us may have life. As the blood which was shed in order to satisfy God's declaration, "Without the shedding of blood there is no forgiveness of sins"

(Hebrews 9:22, N.T.), His blood is able to cleanse us from all sin (1 John 1:7, N.T.).

For Christians, the Passover celebration has been transformed into what is now commonly called the "Lord's Supper" or "Communion Service." This is celebrated by most Christians on a regular basis, as prescribed by the Apostle Paul in 1 Corinthians 11:23-26 (N.T.):

> For I received from the Lord what I also delivered to you, that the Lord Jesus on the night when He was betrayed took bread, and when He had given thanks, He broke it, and said, "This is My body, which is for you. Do this in remembrance of Me." In the same way also He took the cup, after supper, saying, "This cup is the new covenant in My blood. Do this, as often as you drink it, in remembrance of Me." For as often as you eat this bread and drink the cup, you proclaim the Lord's death until He comes.

This is symbolic only. Christians do not actually eat Jesus' flesh nor do they drink His blood. Bread and juice are used regularly to partake in this spiritual celebration of the atoning sacrifice Jesus made by His broken body and His spilled blood for those who believe and are redeemed by faith.

Eating the body of Jesus Christ and drinking His blood, therefore, is enacted by believing, by accepting, and by bringing Him, through faith alone, into one's own life so that He can be the perfect nutrients which are absolutely necessary for having eternal life.

Chapter 22

Jesus: The Testimonies of His Apostles

The Apostles Peter and John were companions of Jesus throughout the days of His ministry on earth. They witnessed His trial; John was at His execution; both visited the tomb after His resurrection; and both watched His ascension to the Father in heaven.

Peter, according to tradition, dictated the story of Jesus to his disciple, Mark. Later, Peter wrote two important, inspired letters to the scattered followers of Jesus. John wrote his testimony in a gospel under his own name. He also wrote inspired letters to other followers of Jesus, plus the book of Revelation.

The Apostle Paul, on the other hand, did not know Jesus while He was upon the earth, but Jesus appeared to Paul afterward in a life-changing vision that led to his conversion and apostleship. Paul's testimony is recorded in the book of the Acts of the Apostles. He went on to write thirteen inspired letters to many newly founded churches, as well as to important followers of Jesus.

Additionally, there is one other testimony, from an unnamed follower of Jesus, who also gave a powerful witness to Jesus through the book of Hebrews. The book of Hebrews is an inspired account of how Jesus fulfilled many prophecies found in the Old Testament.

Let's read what these men wrote, under the inspiration of the Holy Spirit, after Jesus' ascension into heaven. These, of course, will only be selected passages that have to do with our theme of the trail of blood.

Before proceeding to these selections, it is to be noted that the Quran does mention the disciples of Jesus, but not by name. In the only three references in the Quran, it is stated that they believed in God, that they had submitted to God and that they were God's helpers (Q. 3:52, 5:112 and 61:14). The selections below reveal much of what Jesus' disciples really believed.

Selections from the Writings of Apostle Peter

> [K]nowing that you were ransomed from the futile ways inherited from your forefathers, not with perishable things such as silver or gold, but with the precious blood of Christ, like that of a lamb without blemish or spot. He was foreknown before the foundation of the world but was made manifest in these last times for the sake of you, who through Him are believers in God, who raised Him from the dead and gave Him glory, so that your faith and hope are in God.
> 1 Peter 1:18-21 (N.T.)

> He Himself bore our sins in His own body of the tree [the cross], that we might die to sin and live to righteousness. By His wounds you have been

healed. For you were straying like sheep, but have now returned to the Shepherd and Overseer of your souls.
1 Peter 2:24-25 (N.T.)

Selections from the Writings of the Apostle John

My little children, I am writing these things to you so that you may not sin. But if anyone does sin, we have an advocate with the Father, Jesus Christ the righteous. He is the propitiation [the atoning sacrifice] for our sins, and not for ours only but also for the sins of the whole world.
1 John 2:1-2 (N.T.)

In this the love of God was made manifest among us, that God sent His only Son into the world, so that we might live through Him. In this is love, not that we have loved God but that He loved us and sent His Son to be the propitiation for our sins.
1 John 4:9-10 (N.T.)

And I heard a loud voice in heaven, saying, "Now the salvation and the power and the kingdom of our God and the authority of His Christ has come, for the accuser [Satan] of our brothers has been thrown down, who accuses them day and night before our God. And they have conquered him by the blood of the Lamb and by the word of their testimony, for they loved not their lives even unto death."
Revelation 12:10-11 (N.T.)

Selections from the Writings of the Apostle Paul

For while we were still weak, at the right time Christ died for the ungodly...but God shows His love for us in that while we were still sinners, Christ died for us. Since, therefore, we have now been justified by His blood, much more shall we be saved by Him from the wrath of God. For if while we were enemies we were reconciled to God by the death of His Son, much more, now that we are reconciled, shall we be saved by His life. More than that, we also rejoice in God through our Lord Jesus Christ, through whom we have now received reconciliation.
Romans 5:6, 8b-11 (N.T.)

Have this mind among yourselves, which is yours in Christ Jesus, who, though He was in the form of God, did not count equality with God a thing to be grasped, but emptied Himself, by taking the form of a servant, being born in the likeness of men. And being in human form, He humbled Himself by becoming obedient to the point of death, even death on a cross. Therefore, God has highly exalted Him and bestowed on Him the name that is above every name, so that at the name of Jesus every knee should bow, in heaven and on earth and under the earth, and every tongue confess that Jesus Christ is Lord, to the glory of God the Father.
Philippians 2:5-11 (N.T.)

I have been crucified with Christ. It is no longer I who live, but Christ who lives in me. And the life I

now live in the flesh I live by faith in the Son of God, who loved me and gave Himself for me.
Galatians 2:20 (N.T.)

In Him we have redemption through His blood, the forgiveness of our trespasses, according to the riches of His grace...
Ephesians 1:7 (N.T.)

Selections from the Writings in the Book of Hebrews

[W]e see Him who for a little while was made lower than the angels, namely Jesus, crowned with glory and honor because of the suffering of death, so that by the grace of God He might taste death for everyone...that through death He might destroy the one who has the power of death, that is, the devil, and deliver all those who through fear of death were subject to lifelong slavery.
Hebrews 2:9, 14b-15 (N.T.)

Indeed, under the law almost everything is purified with blood, and without the shedding of blood there is no forgiveness of sins.
Hebrews 9:22 (N.T.)

But when Christ had offered for all time a single sacrifice for sins, He sat down at the right hand of God...For by a single offering He has perfected for all times those who are being sanctified [made holy].
Hebrews 10:12, 14 (N.T.)

...looking to Jesus, the Founder and Perfecter of our faith, who for the joy that was set before Him endured the cross, despising the shame, and is seated at the right hand of the throne of God.
Hebrews 12:2 (N.T.)

The accumulated testimonies of the four inspired writers of these selections truly give a strong witness to the transforming power that Jesus had on His immediate followers and all of those who have believed upon Him since.

Chapter 23

Jesus: The Last Adam, the Man From Heaven

Before we move on, it is very important that we clear up one significant misunderstanding[56] with regard to Satan refusing to worship Adam. In the Bible Jesus is referred to as the last Adam. Let's read the passage:

> Thus it is written, "the first man Adam became a living [natural] being"; the last Adam [Jesus] became a life-giving spirit. But it is not the spiritual that is first but the natural [Adam] and then the spiritual [Christ]. The first man [Adam] was from the earth, a man of dust; the second Man [Christ] is from heaven. As was the man of dust, so also those who are of the dust [natural human beings], and as is the Man from heaven, so also are those who are in heaven [the redeemed]. Just as we have borne the image[57] of the man of dust, we shall bear the image of the Man of heaven.
> 1 Corinthians 15:45-49 (N.T.)

Then when we turn to the other key passage that makes all this clear, we read: "And again, when He brings the

---

[56] Please see chapter 6 for more about this.
[57] See chapter "Jesus: Restoring God's Image in Humans."

firstborn[58] into the world, He says, 'Let all God's angels worship Him'" (Hebrews 1:6, N.T.).

These two passages identify Jesus as the "last Adam" in the first passage and as "the firstborn" in the second. So, the Scripture refers to angels worshiping Christ, and this includes Satan. The Quran confused the first Adam with the last Adam (see Q. 2:34; 7:4), that is, Christ.

If we only had a first "Adam," who was only a natural man, all of us would be doomed, as God's wrath and judgment rests on all those born into the fallen, sinful line of Adam. But with the second, or last, "Adam," Jesus, we are given hope for escape from judgment.

---

[58] Jesus is given the highest honor among men. That is the meaning of "firstborn."

Chapter 24

Jesus: Restoring God's Image in Humans

In the Biblical stories of Adam and Eve (Genesis 1:26-27; 5:1, O.T.), and Noah (Genesis 9:6, O.T.) there are explicit references to humans being made in the image of God. But the image of God is not explained in these early stories. Later, in the Old Testament, the image of God is implied when men and women are described as the children of God (Psalm 103:13); and God is described as our Father, for example in the days of Moses (Deuteronomy 32:6, O.T.) and in the writings of Malachi (2:10, O.T.), yet it is not explained.

It was with the appearance of Jesus in human form that this concept of the image of God became prominent again. In the book of Hebrews, we read: "He [Jesus] is the radiance of the glory of God and the exact imprint of His nature" (Hebrews 1:3, N.T.).

God never forgets what He set out to do, namely, to create humans in His own image. Now, because of humanity's fallen nature, the issue is the *re*-creation of humans in the image of God. Jesus phrased it as follows, "Unless one is born again, he cannot see the kingdom of God" (John 3:3, N.T.).

Jesus was able to say this because He solved the problem of man's corrupt nature by becoming the atoning sacrifice for our sin. The Apostle Paul understood the result of this when he wrote, "Therefore, if anyone is in Christ, he is a new creation. The old has passed away; behold, the new has come" (2 Corinthians 5:17, N.T.).

Paul expressed this truth several times in the following passages:

> Just as we have borne the image of the man of dust, we shall also bear the image of the Man of heaven [Christ].
> 1 Corinthians 15:49 (N.T.)

> And we all, with unveiled face, beholding the glory of the Lord, are being transformed into the same image from one degree of glory to another. For this comes from the Lord who is the Spirit.
> 2 Corinthians 3:18 (N.T.)

> [P]ut off your old self, which belongs to our former manner of life and is corrupt through deceitful desires, and be renewed in the spirit of your minds, and put on the new self, created after the likeness of God in true righteousness and holiness.
> Ephesians 4:22-24 (N.T.)

> Do not lie to one another, seeing that you have put off the old self with its practices and have put on the new self, which is being renewed in knowledge after the image of its Creator.
> Colossians 3:9-10 (N.T.)

In the Apostle Peter's second letter to the churches, we read:

> His divine power has granted to us all things that pertain to life and godliness, through the knowledge of Him who called us to His own glory and excellence, by which He has granted to us His precious and very great promises, so that through them you may become partakers of the divine nature, having escaped from the corruption that is in the world because of sinful desire.
> 2 Peter 1:3-4 (N.T.)

Remember what we read in the book of Hebrews 9:22b (N.T.), "Without the shedding of blood [Jesus' blood] there is no forgiveness of sin."

Jesus, by His great sacrifice of Himself on our behalf, removed the barrier of sin between us and God, and made it possible for us to be renewed in the image of our Creator. And having the image of God restored in us, He made it possible for us to fellowship with God our Father.

Chapter 25

Jesus: The Victory of the Lamb

Long before the crucifixion of Jesus, the issue of the reconciliation of the fallen human race with a holy God was settled in the councils of heaven. In the last book of the New Testament, we read: "All the inhabitants of the earth will worship the beast [a representation of Satan]— all whose names have not been written in the book of life belonging to the Lamb [a reference to Christ] that was slain from the creation of the world" (Revelation 13:8, New International Version, N.T.).

God, in His foresight, anticipated the rebellion of Satan in heaven and the subsequent sinfulness of humans on earth, and had planned a way of redeeming us from the consequences of sin. Remember what John the Baptist said as he first met Jesus: "Behold, the Lamb of God, who takes away the sin of the world" (John 1:29, N.T.). And remember the words of the angel Gabriel as he spoke to Joseph, the man engaged to the virgin Mary: "She will bear a Son, and you shall call His name Jesus[59], for He will save His people from their sins" (Matthew 1:21, N.T.).

---

[59] The name "Jesus" means Savior or Deliverer.

Jesus knew He was going to be the supreme sacrificial lamb. He declared this openly to His disciples: "For I have come down from heaven, not to do My own will but the will of Him who sent Me" (John 6:38, N.T.). And He later added, "No one takes it [His life] from Me, but I lay it [His life] down of My own accord. I have authority to lay it down, and I have authority to take it up again [at the resurrection]. This charge I have received from My Father" (John 10:18, N.T.).

Could Jesus have avoided this terrible pain of crucifixion if He had wanted to? Yes, but He did not. In reply to His disciples who tried to prevent His arrest, He said, "Do you think that I cannot appeal to My Father, and He will at once send Me more than twelve legions of angels? But how then should the Scriptures be fulfilled, that it must be so?" (Matthew 26:53-54, N.T.).

Jesus knew what He was getting into that last week of His life. He was going to face the Roman government that was occupying the nation of Israel. He would be falsely charged with treason, that is, of setting up a political kingdom to rival the power of Rome. The puppet king Herod would conspire with Rome to crucify Jesus. The Jewish religious leaders would call for Jesus' execution because they were jealous of His popularity. The mobs of common people were roused by their rulers to cry for Jesus' crucifixion. Knowing all this, Jesus, nevertheless, was determined to carry out God's plan. In Luke 9:51 (N.T.), we read of Jesus: "When the days drew near for Him to be taken up [on a cross], He set His face to go to Jerusalem."

Have you ever imagined yourself in Jesus' shoes and wondered what was going through His mind as He faced the unbelievable cruelty of death by crucifixion? Did He see what was beyond His death and resurrection? Yes, He did. We read in the New Testament book of Hebrews this beautiful glimpse of His thoughts: "[L]ooking to Jesus, the Founder and Perfecter of our faith, who for the joy that was set before Him endured the cross, despising the shame, and is seated at the right hand of the throne of God" (Hebrews 12:2, N.T.).

What was that joy He looked forward to? Here are three facets of that joy:

Jesus successfully died on the cross as a victim-sacrifice, as the "Lamb of God," for the sins of the whole world. As a mere man, His life would not have been sufficient for all; but as the Son of God, His blood would be of infinite worth. Just think about it: by satisfying the justice of God on behalf of rebellious humankind, He opened the door of forgiveness for all who truly repent and believe in Jesus as their Savior and Lord.

Jesus also disarmed Satan, the accuser of sinners. Satan knew about the Law of Moses. He knew about the sentence of death passed on all who sinned. He acted like a prosecuting attorney in condemning sinners. Jesus, by paying the penalty for all, rendered Satan powerless. He brought believers out of Satan's power and safely into the Kingdom of God.

Finally, by rising from the dead, three days after the crucifixion, Jesus conquered death personally and for all who believed in Him.[60] In other words, by His death and resurrection, He offered new life to all.

Jesus, the Lamb of God, was victorious over all three of humankind's enemies: sin, Satan and death. That is why we read of the Lamb's victory in these words:

> And they sang a new song, saying,
> "Worthy are You [the Lamb] to take the scroll and to open its seals,
> for You were slain, and by Your blood You ransomed people for God
> from every tribe and language and people and nation,
> and You have made them a kingdom and priests to our God,
> and they shall reign on the earth."
> Revelation 5:9-10 (N.T.)

There were also thousands and thousands of angels "saying with a loud voice, 'Worthy is the Lamb who was slain, to receive power and wealth and wisdom and might and honor and glory and blessing!'" (Revelation 5:12, N.T.).

And in a later scene, we read:

> [T]hey sing...the song of the Lamb, saying,
> "Great and amazing are Your deeds,
> O Lord God Almighty!
> Just and true are Your ways,

---

[60] In Quran 4:158, there is a reference to Jesus' ascension, in these words, "And Allah raised him [Jesus] up unto Himself..." That is the only reference in the Quran to Jesus' status in heaven.

O King of the nations!
Who will not fear, O Lord,
and glorify Your name?
For You alone are holy.
All nations will come
and worship You,
for Your righteous acts
have been revealed."
Revelation 15:3-4[61] (N.T.)

As the victorious Lamb who is God, Jesus appeared to the Apostle John, who probably knew Him best while He was here on earth, and yet when John encountered Him, John "fell at His feet as though dead." It is important that you now envision that this victorious Lamb is no longer simply a sacrificial lamb. We are presented with a completely new image of Jesus Christ, who now lives in heaven:

> Then I turned to see the voice that was speaking to me, and on turning I saw...One like a Son of Man, clothed with a long robe and with a golden sash around His chest. The hairs of His head were white, like white wool, like snow. His eyes were like a flame of fire, His feet were like burnished bronze, refined in a furnace, and His voice was like the roar of many waters. In His right hand He held seven stars, from His mouth came a sharp two-edged sword, and His face was like the sun shining in full strength.

---

[61] For the interested reader, there is page after page in the New Testament book of Revelation about Jesus' activity in heaven. We have selected only a few quotes from the book of Revelation to stimulate your appetite for reading a fuller portrayal of Jesus' activity as "the Lamb who is victorious."

When I saw Him, I fell at His feet as though dead. But He laid His right hand on me, saying, "Fear not, I am the First and the Last, and the Living One. I died, and behold I am alive forevermore, and I have the keys of Death and Hades [hell]."
Revelation 1:12-18 (N.T.)

Chapter 26

Conclusion

And We ransomed him with a mighty sacrifice...
Q. 37:107

"God will provide for Himself the lamb for a burnt offering..."
Genesis 22:8 (O.T.)

As you may remember, we opened this book with these two verses. Throughout this entire book, as we have been tracing the trail of blood from Adam to the throne of God, we have been grappling with the meaning of these verses from the Quran, and Genesis in the Bible.

In the story of Abraham's obedience in offering Isaac as a sacrifice, God intervened and provided a ram for sacrifice instead. By faith, Abraham, on the way up the mountain with Isaac spoke prophetic words about Jesus when he said, "God will provide for Himself the lamb..."

Abraham was willing to sacrifice his own son in obedience to God's command. God Himself offered His own Son, Jesus, in order to provide for the forgiveness of sins for all who believe in that holy, perfect and mighty substitutionary sacrifice.

Ultimately, there is only one answer that resolves all the questions about what God requires in order to redeem each of us from ever going to hell, enabling us to become His children.

God has already offered His son, Jesus Christ, as *the* mighty sacrifice that is powerful enough to atone for all the sin ever committed by people throughout all of time.

God Himself provided *the* Lamb, Jesus Christ, whose blood was shed for the forgiveness of all sin.

Jesus' blood was holy, without sin or impurity. Because God declared, "Without the shedding of blood, there is no forgiveness of sin" (Hebrews 9:22, N.T.), He alone had to provide a perfect, mighty, sacrificial Lamb that fully met all His holy requirements for the complete forgiveness of sin.

As a summary of all that we've presented in this book, and so that you may clearly see what God is waiting for you to do with this new understanding, please consider the following verses from the Bible:

> For they [the crowd] asked [Jesus], "What must we do, to be doing the works of God?" Jesus answered them, "This is the work of God, that you believe in Him whom He has sent."
> John 6:28-29 (N.T.)

> "For God so loved the world, that He gave His only Son, that whosoever believes in Him should not perish but have eternal life."
> John 3:16 (N.T.)

And this is the testimony, that God gave us eternal life, and this life is in His Son. Whoever has the Son has life, and whoever does not have the Son of God does not have life. I write these things to you who believe in the name of the Son of God that you may *know* that you have eternal life.
1 John 5:11-13 (N.T., emphasis added)

Now that you have completed this journey with us down the trail of blood from Adam to the throne of Jesus Christ, you now must decide whether or not you believe.

Do you believe that Jesus' sacrifice of His blood is able to atone for your own sins, and that by believing this truth and repenting of your sinful life, you will be saved from judgment and punishment?

God offers the free gift of salvation for you even now.

What will you do?

Appendix A

Names of Prophets that Are Common to the Quran and the Bible

Originally these names appeared long ago in Hebrew and Greek. More recently these names appear in Arabic in the Quran. From all three languages these names have come into English. Since they appear differently, we will match them up and list them chronologically in history.

Biblical Name	Description	Quranic Name
Adam	The first man	*Adam*
Cain	Adam's first son	*Qabeel*
Abel	Adam's second son	*Habeel*
Noah	The flood	*Nuh*
Abraham	The father of all	*Ibrahim*
Lot	Abraham's nephew	*Lut*
Ishmael	Abraham's son	*Ismail*
Isaac	Abraham's son	*Ishaq*
Jacob	Isaac's son	*Yaqoob*
Joseph	Jacob's son	*Yusuf*
Job	Arab king	*Ayyub*
Aaron	Moses' older brother	*Haroon*
Moses	The great lawgiver	*Musa*
David	A great king	*Dawood*
Solomon	David's son	*Suleiman*

Elijah	A great prophet	*Ilyas*
Elisha	Anointed by Elijah	*Al Yasa*
Jonah	Prophet to Nineveh	*Yunus*
Isaiah	(Not found by name in the Quran)	
Ezra	A priest of Israel	*Uzair*
Zachariah	Father of John the Prophet/Baptist	*Zakariya*
John	The Prophet/Baptist	*Yahya*
Mary	The virgin mother	*Miriam*
Jesus	Savior, Deliverer	*Isa*
Messiah	Anointed One	*Masih*

Other Words that Are Important to Know

English Term	Meaning	Quranic Term
Christian	Believers in Jesus	*Nasara*
The Gospel	Means "good news"	*Injil*
Torah	Law of Moses	*Tauret*
Psalms	Songs of David	*Zabur*
Jews	Jewish people	*Yehudi*
The Prophets	Named and unnamed	*Unbiya*
Satan	The Adversary	*Shaitan*
The Devil	The Deceiver	*Iblis*

Appendix B

Books of the Bible
(In the order in which they appear)

The Old Testament
Genesis
Exodus
Leviticus
Numbers
Deuteronomy
Joshua
Judges
Ruth
1 Samuel
2 Samuel
1 Kings
2 Kings
1 Chronicles
2 Chronicles
Ezra
Nehemiah
Esther
Job
Psalms
Proverbs
Ecclesiastes
Song of Solomon

Isaiah
Jeremiah
Lamentations
Ezekiel
Daniel
Hosea
Joel
Amos
Obadiah
Jonah
Micah
Nahum
Habakkuk
Zephaniah
Haggai
Zechariah
Malachi

The New Testament
Matthew
Mark
Luke
John
Acts (of the Apostles)
Romans
1 Corinthians
2 Corinthians
Galatians
Ephesians
Philippians
Colossians
1 Thessalonians
2 Thessalonians
1 Timothy

2 Timothy
Titus
Philemon
Hebrews
James
1 Peter
2 Peter
1 John
2 John
3 John
Jude
Revelation

Index of Scriptures and Quranic References